Alfred Denis Godley

Aspects of Modern Oxford

Alfred Denis Godley

Aspects of Modern Oxford

ISBN/EAN: 9783743331457

Manufactured in Europe, USA, Canada, Australia, Japa

Cover: Foto ©ninafisch / pixelio.de

Manufactured and distributed by brebook publishing software
(www.brebook.com)

Alfred Denis Godley

Aspects of Modern Oxford

CONTENTS

CHAP.		PAGE
I.	OF DONS AND COLLEGES	1
II.	OF UNDERGRADUATES	17
III.	OF SIGHTSEERS	35
IV.	OF EXAMINATIONS	51
V.	UNIVERSITY JOURNALISM	74
VI.	THE UNIVERSITY AS SEEN FROM OUTSIDE	88
VII.	DIARY OF A DON	105
VIII.	THE UNIVERSITY AS A PLACE OF LEARNED LEISURE	120

LIST OF ILLUSTRATIONS

IN CORNMARKET STREET. By *T. H. Crawford.*	*Frontispiece*
IN CHRISTCHURCH CATHEDRAL. By *J. H. Lorimer* .	P. 2
NEW COLLEGE, OXFORD. By *E. Stamp*	6
CORPUS CHRISTI COLLEGE. By *J. H. Lorimer* . .	10
SMOKING-ROOM AT THE UNION. By *T. H. Crawford.*	14
CRICKET IN THE PARKS. By *L. Speed*	22
WAITING FOR THE COX. By *L. Speed*	26
RINGOAL IN NEW COLLEGE. By *L. Speed.* . . .	29
GOLF AT OXFORD. THE PLATEAU HOLE AND ARNOLD'S TREE. By *L. Speed*	32
COMMEMORATION : OUTSIDE THE SHELDONIAN THEATRE. By *T. H. Crawford*	38
IN COLLEGE ROOMS. By *T. H. Crawford*	40
A BALL AT CHRISTCHURCH. By *T. H. Crawford* .	42
THE DEER PARK, MAGDALEN COLLEGE, OXFORD. By *J. H. Lorimer.*	46
IN CONVOCATION : CONFERRING A DEGREE. By *E. Stamp*	48

LIST OF ILLUSTRATIONS

	PAGE
A LECTURE-ROOM IN MAGDALEN COLLEGE. *By E. Stamp*	52
THE LIBRARY, MERTON COLLEGE. *By E. Stamp*	62
READING THE NEWDIGATE. *By T. H. Crawford*	66
A DANCE AT ST. JOHN'S. *By T. H. Crawford*	72
THE RADCLIFFE. *By E. Stamp*	76
IN THE BODLEIAN. *By E. Stamp*	80
SAILING ON THE UPPER RIVER. *By L. Speed*	86
PORCH OF ST. MARY'S. *By J. Pennell*	90
IN EXETER COLLEGE CHAPEL. *By E. Stamp*	94
PARSONS' PLEASURE. *By L. Speed*	102
FENCING. *By L. Speed*	103
LAWN TENNIS AT OXFORD. *By L. Speed*	114
BOWLS IN NEW COLLEGE GARDEN. *By L. Speed*	120
COACHING THE EIGHT. *By J. H. Lorimer*	132
EVENING ON THE RIVER. *By E. Stamp*	134

ASPECTS OF MODERN OXFORD

I

OF DONS AND COLLEGES

'We ain't no thin red heroes, nor we ain't no blackguards too,
But single men in barracks, most remarkable like you.'
Rudyard Kipling.

FELLOWS of Colleges who travel on the continent of Europe have, from time to time, experienced the almost insuperable difficulty of explaining to the more or less intelligent foreigner their own reason of existence, and that of the establishment to which they are privileged to belong. It is all the worse if your neighbour at the *table d'hôte* is acquainted with the Universities of his own country, for these offer no parallel at all, and to attempt to illustrate by means of them is not only futile but misleading. Define any college according to the general scheme indicated by its founder; when you have made the situation as intelligible as a limited knowledge of French or German will allow, the inquirer will conclude that '*also* it is a monastic institution,' and that you are wearing a hair shirt under your tourist tweeds. Try to disabuse him of this impression by pointing out that colleges do not compel to celibacy, and are intended mainly for the instruction of youth, and your Continental will go away with the conviction that an English University is composed of a conglomeration of public schools. If he tries to get further information from the conversation of a casual undergraduate, it will appear that a *Ruderverein* on the Danube offers most points of comparison.

Fellows themselves fare no better, and are left in an — if possible — darker obscurity. That they are in some way connected with education is tolerably obvious, but the particular nature of the connexion is unexplained. Having thoroughly confused the subject by showing inconclusively that you are neither a monk, nor a schoolmaster, nor a *Privat Docent*, you probably acquiesce from sheer weariness in the title of *Professor*, which, perhaps, is as convenient as any other; and, after all, *Professoren* are very different from Professors. But all this does nothing to elucidate the nature of a College. To do this abroad is nearly as hard as to define the function of a University in England.

For even at home the general uneducated public, taking but a passing interest in educational details, is apt to be hopelessly at sea as to the mutual relation of Colleges and Universities. In the public mind the College probably represents the University : an Oxonian will be sometimes spoken of as 'at College ;' University officials are confused with heads of houses, and Collections with University examinations. That foundation which is consecrated to the education of Welsh Oxonians is generally referred to in the remote fastnesses of the Cymru as Oxford College. As usual, a concrete material object, palpable and visible, is preferred before a cold abstraction like the University. Explain to the lay mind that a University is an aggregate of Colleges: it is not, of course, but the definition will serve sometimes. Then how about the London University, which is an examining body? And how does it happen that there is a University College in Oxford, not to mention another in Gower Street? and that Trinity College across the water is often called Dublin University? All these problems are calculated to leave the inquirer very much where he was at first, and in him who tries to explain them to shake the firm foundations of Reason.

It may be a truism, but it is nevertheless true—according to a phrase which has done duty in the Schools ere now—that the history of the University is, and has been for the last five hundred years, the history of its Colleges; and it is also true that the interweaving of Collegiate with University life has very much complicated the question of the student's reason of existence. We do not, of course, know what may have been the various motives which prompted the bold baron, or squire, or yeoman of the twelfth or thirteenth century to send the most clerkly or least muscular of his sons to herd with his fellows in the crowded streets or the mean hostelries of pre-collegiate Oxford; nor have we very definite data as to the kind of life which the scholar of the family lived when he got there. Perhaps he resided in a 'hall;' according to some authorities there were as many as three hundred halls in the days of Edward I.; perhaps he was master of his own destinies, like the free and independent unattached student of modern days— minus a Censor to watch over the use of his liberties. But what is tolerably certain is that he did not then come to Oxford so much with the intention of 'having a good time' as with the desire of improving his mind, or, at least, in some way or other taking part in the intellectual life of the period, which then centred in the University. It might be that among the throngs of boys and young men who crowded the straitened limits of mediaeval

Oxford, there were many who supported the obscure tenets of their particular Doctor Perspicuus against their opponents' Doctor Inexplicabilis rather with bills and bows than with disputations in the Schools; but every Oxonian was in some way vowed to the advancement of learning—at least, it is hard to see what other inducement there was to face what must have been, even with all due allowance made, the exceptional hardships of a student's life. Then came the Colleges—University dating from unknown antiquity, although the legend which connects its foundation with Alfred has now shared the fate of most legends; Balliol and Merton, at the end of the thirteenth century; and the succeeding centuries were fruitful in the establishment of many other now venerable foundations, taking example and encouragement from the success and reputation of their earlier compeers. In their original form colleges were probably intended to be places of quiet retirement and study, where the earnest scholar might peacefully pursue his researches without fear of disturbance by the wilder spirits who roamed the streets and carried on the traditional feuds of Town and Gown or of North and South.

By a curious reverse of circumstances the collegian and the '*scholaris nulli collegio vel aulae ascriptus*' of modern days seem to have changed characters For I have heard it said by those who have to do with college discipline that their *alumni* are no longer invariably distinguished by 'a gentle nature and studious habits' — qualities for which, as the Warden of Merton says, colleges were originally intended to provide a welcome haven of rest, and which are now the especial and gratifying characteristics of that whilom roisterer and boon companion, the Unattached Student.

We have it on the authority of historians that the original collegiate design was, properly speaking, a kind of model lodging-house; an improved, enlarged, and strictly supervised edition of the many hostels where the primitive undergraduate did mostly congregate. Fellows and scholars alike were to be studious and discreet persons; the seniors were to devote themselves to research, and to stand in a quasi-parental or elder-brotherly relation to the juniors who had not yet attained to the grade of a Baccalaureus. Very strict rules—probably based on those of monastic institutions— governed the whole body: rules, however, which are not unnecessarily severe when we consider the fashion of the age and the comparative youth of both fellows and scholars. Many scholars must have been little more than children, and the junior don of the fifteenth century may often have been young enough to receive that corporal punishment which our rude forefathers inflicted even on the gentler sex.

> 'Solomon said, in accents mild,
> Spare the rod and spoil the child;
> Be they man or be they maid,
> Whip 'em and wallop 'em, Solomon said'

—and the sage's advice was certainly followed in the case of scholars, who were birched for offences which in these latter days would call down a 'gate,' a fine, or an imposition. Authorities tell us that the early fellow might even in certain cases be mulcted of his dress, a penalty which is now reserved for Irish patriots in gaol; and it would seem that his consumption of beer was limited by regulations which would now be intolerable to his scout. Some of the details respecting crime and punishment, which have been preserved in ancient records, are of the most remarkable description. A former Fellow of Corpus (so we are informed by Dr. Fowler's History of that College) who had been proved guilty of an over-susceptibility to the charms of beauty, was condemned as a penance to preach eight sermons in the Church of St. Peter-in-the-East. Such was the inscrutable wisdom of a bygone age.

Details have altered since then, but the general scheme of college discipline remains much the same. Even in the days when practice was slackest, theory retained its ancient stringency. When Mr. Gibbon of Magdalen absented himself from his lectures, his excuses were received 'with an indulgent smile;' when he desired to leave Oxford for a few days, he appears to have done so without let or hindrance; but both residence and attendance at lectures were theoretically necessary. The compromise was hardly satisfactory, but as the scholars' age increased and the disciplinary rule meant for fourteen had to be applied to eighteen, what was to be done? So, too, we are informed that in the days of our fathers undergraduates endured a Procrustean tyranny. So many chapel services you must attend; so many lectures you must hear, connected or not with your particular studies; and there was no relaxation of the rule; no excuse even of 'urgent business' would serve the pale student who wanted to follow the hounds or play in a cricket match. Things, in fact, would have been at a deadlock had not the authorities recognised the superiority of expediency to mere morality, and invariably accepted without question the plea of ill-health. To 'put on an *aeger*' when in the enjoyment of robust health was after all as justifiable

CORPUS CHRISTI COLLEGE.
Drawn by J. H. Lorimer.

a fiction as the 'not at home' of ordinary society. You announced yourself as too ill to go to a lecture, and then rode with the Bicester or played cricket to your heart's content. This remarkable system is now practically obsolete; perhaps we are more moral.

Modern collegiate discipline is a parlous matter. There are still the old problems to be faced—the difficulty of adapting old rules to new conditions—the danger on the one hand of treating boys too much like men, and on the other of treating men too much like boys. Hence college authorities generally fall back on some system of more or less ingenious compromise—a course which is no doubt prudent in the long run, and shows a laudable desire for the attainment of the Aristotelian 'mean,' but which, like most compromises, manages to secure the disapproval alike of all shades of outside opinion. We live with the fear of the evening papers before our eyes, and an erring undergraduate who has been sent down may quite possibly be avenged by a newspaper column reflecting on college discipline in general, and the dons who sent him down in particular. Every day martinets tell us that the University is going to the dogs from excess of leniency; while critics of the 'Boys-will-be-boys' school point out the extreme danger of sitting permanently on the safety valve, and dancing on the edge of an active volcano.

In recent years most of the 'Halls' have been practically extinguished, and thereby certain eccentricities of administration removed from our midst. It was perhaps as well; some of these ancient and honourable establishments having during the present century rather fallen from their former reputation, from their readiness to receive into the fold incapables or minor criminals to whom the moral or intellectual atmosphere of a college was uncongenial. This was a very convenient system for colleges, who could thus get rid of an idle or stupid man without the responsibility of blighting his University career and his prospects in general; but the Halls, which were thus turned into a kind of sink, became rather curious and undesirable abiding-places in consequence. They were inhabited by grave and reverend seniors who couldn't, and by distinguished athletes who wouldn't, pass Smalls, much less Mods. At one time 'Charsley's' was said to be able to play the 'Varsity Eleven. These mixed multitudes appear to have been governed on very various and remarkable principles. At one establishment it was considered a breach of courtesy if you did not, when going to London, give the authorities some idea of the *probable* length of your absence. 'The way to govern a college,' the venerated head of this institution is reported to have said, 'is this—*to keep one eye shut*,' presumably the optic on the side of the offender. Yet it is curious that while most of the Halls appear to have been ruled rather by the *gant de velours* than the *main de fer*, one of them is currently reported to have been the scene of an attempt to inflict corporal punishment. This heroic endeavour to restore the customs of the ancients was not crowned with immediate success, and he who should have been beaten with stripes fled for justice to the Vice-Chancellor's Court.

Casual visitors to Oxford who are acquainted with the statutes of the University will no doubt have observed that it has been found unnecessary to insist on exact obedience to all the rules which were framed for the student of four hundred years ago. For instance, boots are generally worn; undergraduates are not prohibited from riding horses, nor even from carrying lethal weapons; the *herba nicotiana sive Tobacco* is in common use; and, especially in summer, garments are not so 'subfusc' as the strict letter of the law requires. Perhaps, too, the wearing of the academic cap and gown is not so universally necessary as it was heretofore. All these are matters for the jurisdiction of the Proctors, who rightly lay more stress on the real order and good behaviour of their realm. And whatever evils civilisation may bring in the train, there can be no doubt that the task of these officials is far less dangerous than of old, as their subjects are less turbulent. They have no

SMOKING-ROOM AT THE UNION.
Drawn by T. H. Crawford.

longer to interfere in the faction fights of Northern and Southern students. It is unusual for a Proctor to carry a pole-axe, even when he is 'drawing' the most dangerous of billiard-rooms. The Town and Gown rows which used to provide so attractive a picture for the novelist — where the hero used to stand pale and determined, defying a crowd of infuriated bargemen — are extinct and forgotten these last ten years. Altogether the streets are quieter; models, in fact, of peace and good order: when the anarchical element is loose it seems to prefer the interior of Colleges. Various reasons might be assigned for this: sometimes the presence of too easily defied authority gives a piquancy to crime; or it is the place itself which is the incentive. The open space of a quadrangle is found to be a convenient stage for the performance of the midnight reveller. He is watched from the windows by a ring of admiring friends, and the surrounding walls are a kind of sounding-board which enhances the natural beauty of 'Ta-ra-ra-boom-de-ay' (with an accompaniment of tea-tray and poker *obbligato*). Every one has his own ideal of an enjoyable evening.

II

OF UNDERGRADUATES

> 'In the sad and sodden street
> To and fro
> Flit the feverstricken feet
> Of the Freshers, as they meet,
> Come and go.'

WHATEVER the theory of their founders, it is at no late period in the history of colleges that we begin to trace the development of the modern undergraduate. It was only natural that the 'gentle natures and studious habits' of a select band of learners should undergo some modification as college after college was founded, and comparative frivolity would from time to time obtain admission to the sacred precincts. The University became the resort of wealth and rank, as well as of mere intellect, and the gradual influx of commoners—still more, of 'gentlemen commoners'—once for all determined the character of colleges as places of serious and uninterrupted study. Probably the Civil War, bringing the Court to Oxford, was a potent factor in relaxation of the older academic discipline; deans or sub-wardens of the period doubtless finding some difficulty in adapting their rules to the requirements of undergraduates who might from time to time absent themselves from chapel or lecture in order to raid a Parliamentary outpost.

But perhaps the most instructive picture of the seventeenth-century undergraduate is to be found in the account-book of one Wilding, of Wadham (published by the Oxford Historical Society), apparently a reading man and a scholar of his college, destined for Holy Orders. The number of his books (he gives a list of them) shows him to have been something of a student, while repeated entries of large sums paid for 'Wiggs' (on one occasion as much as 14s.—more than his 'Battles' for the quarter!) would seem to suggest something of the habits of the 'gay young sparks' alluded to by Hearne in the next century. On the whole, Master Wilding appears to have been a virtuous and studious young gentleman. Now and then the natural man asserts himself, and he treats his friends to wine or 'coffea,' or even makes an excursion to 'Abbington' (4s.!). Towards the end of his career a 'gaudy' costs 2s. 6d., after which comes the too-suggestive entry, 'For a purge, 1s.' Then comes the close: outstanding bills are paid to the alarming extent of 7s. 8d.; a 'wigg,' which originally cost 14s., is disposed of at a ruinous reduction for 6s.—the prudent man does not give it away to his scout—and J. Wilding, B.A., e. Coll., Wadh., retires to his country parsonage—having first invested sixpence in a sermon. Evidently a person of methodical habits and punctual payments; that had two wigs, and everything handsome about him; and that probably grumbled quite as much at the 10s. fee for his tutor as his modern successor does at his 8l. 6s. 8d. But, on the whole, collegiate and university fees seem to have been small.

After this description of the *vie intime* of an undergraduate at Wadham, history is reserved on the subject of the junior members of the University; which is the more disappointing, as the historic Muse is not only garrulous, but exceedingly scandalous in recounting the virtues and the aberrations of eighteenth-century dons. Here and there we find an occasional notice of the ways of undergraduates — here a private memoir, there an academic *brochure*. We learn, incidentally, how Mr. John Potenger, of New College, made 'theams in prose and verse,' and eventually 'came to a tollerable proficiency in colloquial Latin;' how Mr. Meadowcourt, of Merton, got into serious trouble—was prevented, in fact, from taking his degree—for drinking the health of His Majesty King George the First; and how Mr. Carty, of University College, suffered a similar fate 'for prophaning, with mad intemperance, that day, on which he ought, with sober chearfulness, to have commemorated the restoration of King Charles the Second' (this was in 1716); how Mr.

Shenstone found, at Pembroke College, both sober men 'who amused themselves in the evening with reading Greek and drinking water,' and also 'a set of jolly sprightly young fellows . . . . who drank ale, smoked tobacco,' and even 'punned;' and how Lord Shelburne had a 'narrow - minded tutor.' From which we may gather, that University life was not so very different from what it is now: our forefathers were more exercised about politics, for which we have now substituted a perhaps extreme devotion to athletics. But for the most part, the undergraduate is not prominent in history—seeming, in fact, to be regarded as the least important element in the University. On the other hand, his successor of the present century— the era of the Examination Schools—occupies so prominent a place in the eyes of the public that it is difficult to speak of him, lest haply one should be accused of frivolity or want of reverence for the *raison d'être* of all academic institutions.

His own reason of existence is not so

obvious. It was, as we have said, tolerably clear that the mediaeval student came to Oxford primarily for the love of learning something, at any rate; but the student *fin de siècle* is one of the most labyrinthine parts of a complex civilisation. Of the hundreds of boys who are shot on the G.W R. platform every October to be caressed or kicked by Alma Mater, and returned in due time full or empty, it is only an insignificant minority who come up with the ostensible purpose of learning. Their reasons are as many as the colours of their portmanteaus. Brown has come up because he is in the sixth form at school, and was sent in for a scholarship by a head-master desiring an advertisement; Jones, because it is thought by his friends that he might get into the 'Varsity eleven; Robinson, because his father considers a University career to be a stepping-stone to the professions — which it fortunately is not as yet. Mr. Sangazur is going to St. Boniface because his father was there; and Mr. J. Sangazur Smith — well, probably because *his* father wasn't. Altogether

CRICKET IN THE PARKS. By Lancelot Speed.

they are a motley crew, and it is not the least achievement of the University that she does somehow or other manage to impress a certain stamp on so many different kinds of metal. But in this she is only an instrument in the hands of modern civilisation, which is always extinguishing eccentricities and abnormal types; and even Oxford, while her sons are getting rid of those interesting individualities which used to distinguish them from each other, is fast losing many of the peculiarities which used to distinguish it from the rest of the world. It is an age of monotony. Even the Freshman, that delightful creation of a bygone age, is not by any means what he was. He is still young, but no longer innocent; the bloom is off his credulity; you cannot play practical jokes upon him any more. Now and then a young man will present himself to his college authorities in a gown of which the superfluous dimensions and unusual embroidery betray the handiwork of the provincial tailor; two or three neophytes may annually be seen perambulating the High in academic dress with a walking-stick; but these are only survivals. Senior men have no longer their old privileges of 'ragging' the freshman. In ancient times, as we are informed by the historian of Merton College, 'Freshmen were expected to sit on a form, and make jokes for the amusement of their companions, on pain of being "tucked," or scarified by the thumb-nail applied under the lip. The first Earl of Shaftesbury describes in detail this rather barbarous jest as practised at Exeter College, and relates how, aided by some freshmen of unusual size and strength, he himself headed a mutiny which led to the eventual abolition of 'tucking.' Again, on Candlemas Day every freshman received notice to prepare a speech to be delivered on the following Shrove Tuesday, when they were compelled to declaim in undress from a form placed on the high table, being rewarded with "cawdel" if the performances were good, with cawdel and salted drink if it were indifferent, and with salted drink and "tucks" if it were dull.' This is what American students call 'hazing,' and the German *Fuchs* is subjected to similar ordeals. But we have changed all that, and treat the 'fresher' now with the respect he deserves.

Possibly the undergraduate of fiction and the drama may have been once a living reality. But he is so no more, and modern realistic novelists will have to imagine some hero less crude in colouring and more in harmony with the compromises and neutral tints of the latter half of the nineteenth century. The young Oxonian or Cantab of fifty years back, as represented by contemporary or nearly contemporary writers, was always in extremes:—

'When he was good he was very, very good;
But when he was bad he was horrid,'

like the little girl of the poet. He was either an inimitable example of improbable virtue, or abnormally vicious. The bad undergraduate defied the Ten Commandments, all and severally, with the ease and success of the villain of transpontine melodrama. Nothing came amiss to him, from forgery to screwing up the Dean and letting it be understood that some one else had done it; but retribution generally came at last, and this compound of manifold vices was detected and rusticated; and it was understood that from rustication to the gallows was the shortest and easiest of transitions. The virtuous undergraduate wore trousers too short for him and supported his relations. He did not generally join in any athletic pastimes, but when the stroke of his college eight fainted from excitement just before the start, the neglected sizar threw off his threadbare coat, leapt into the vacant seat, and won his crew at once the proud position of head of the river by the simple process of making four bumps on the same night, explaining afterwards that he had practised in a dingey and saw how it could be done. Then there was the Admirable Crichton of University life, perhaps the commonest type among these heroes of romance. He was invariably at Christ Church, and very often had a background of more or less tragic memories from

WAITING FOR THE COX. Drawn by Lancelot Speed.

the far-away days of his *jeunesse orageuse*. Nevertheless he unbent so far as to do nothing much during the first three and a half years of his academic career, except to go to a good many wine parties, where he always wore his cap and gown (especially in female fiction), and drank more than any one else. Then, when every one supposed he must be ploughed in Greats, he sat up so late for a week, and wore so many wet towels, that eventually he was announced at the Encaenia, amid the plaudits of his friends and the approving smiles of the Vice-Chancellor, as the winner of a Double-First, several University prizes, and a Fellowship ; after which it was only right and natural that the recipient of so many coveted distinctions should lead the heroine of the piece to the altar.

Possibly the Oxford of a bygone generation may have furnished models for these brilliantly coloured pictures ; or, as is more probable, they were created by the licence of fiction. At any rate the 'man' of modern times is a far less picturesque person — unpicturesque

even to the verge of becoming ordinary. He
is seldom eccentric or *outré* in externals. His
manners are such as he has learnt at school,
and his customs those of the world he lives in.
His dress would excite no remark in Piccadilly.
The gorgeous waistcoats of Leech's pencil and
Calverley's '*crurum non enarrabile tegmen*'
belong to ancient history. He is, on the
whole, inexpensive in his habits, as it is now
the fashion to be poor; he no longer orders
in a tailor's whole shop, and his clubs are
generally managed with economy and prudence.
If, however, the undergraduate occasionall
displays the virtues of maturer age, there are
certain indications that he is less of a grown-
up person than he was in the brave days of
old. It takes him a long time to forget his
school-days. Only exceptionally untrammelled
spirits regard independent reading as more
important than the ministrations of their tutor.
Pass-men have been known to speak of their
work for the schools as 'lessons,' and, in their
first term, to call the head of the College the
head-master. Naturally, too, school-life has

RINGOAL IN NEW COLLEGE.
Drawn by Lancelot Speed.

imbued both Pass and Class men with an enduring passion for games—probably rather a good thing in itself, although inadequate as the be-all and end-all of youthful energy. Even those who do not play them can talk

about them. Cricket and football are always as prolific a topic as the weather, and nearly as interesting, as many a perfunctory 'Fresher's breakfast' can testify.

The undergraduate, in these as in other things, is like the young of his species, with whom, after all, he has a good deal in common. Take, in short, the ordinary provincial young man; add a dash of the schoolboy and just a touch of the *Bursch*, and you have what Mr. Hardy calls the 'Normal Undergraduate.'

It used to be the custom to draw a very hard-and-fast line of demarcation between the rowing and the reading man — rowing being taken as a type of athletics in general, and indeed being the only form of physical exercise which possessed a regular organization. Rumour has it that a certain tutor (now defunct) laid so much emphasis on this distinction that men whose circumstances permitted them to be idle were regarded with disfavour if they took to reading. He docketed freshmen as reading or non-reading men, and would not allow either kind to stray into the domain of the other. However, the general fusion of classes and professions has levelled these boundaries now. The rowing man reads to a certain extent, and the reading man has very often pretensions to athletic eminence; it is in fact highly desirable that he should, now that a 'Varsity 'blue' provides an assistant master in a school with at least as good a salary as does a brilliant degree. Yet, although the great majority of men belong to the intermediate class of those who take life as they find it, and make no one occupation the object of their exclusive devotion, it is hardly necessary to say that there are still extremes—the Brutal Athlete at one end of the line and the bookish recluse (often, though wrongly, identified with the 'Smug') at the other. The existence of the first is encouraged by the modern tendency to professionalism in athletics. Mere amateurs who regard games as an amusement can never hope to do anything; a thing must be taken seriously. Every schoolboy who wishes to obtain renown in the columns of sporting papers has his 'record,' and comes up to Oxford with the express intention of 'cutting' somebody else's, and the athletic authorities of the University know all about Jones's bowling average at Eton, or Brown's form as three-quarter-back at Rugby, long before these distinguished persons have matriculated. Nor is it only cricket, football, and rowing that are the objects of our worship. Even so staid and contemplative a pastime as golf ranks among 'athletics;' and perhaps in time the authorities will be asked to give a 'Blue' for croquet. These things being so, on the whole, perhaps, we should be grateful to the eminent athlete for the comparative affability of his demeanour, so long as he is not seriously contradicted. He is great, but he is generally merciful.

Thews and sinews have probably as much admiration as is good for them, and nearly as much as they want. On the other hand, the practice of reading has undoubtedly been popularised. It is no longer a clique of students who seek honours; public opinion in and outside the University demands of an increasing majority of men that they should appear to be improving their minds. The Pass-man pure and simple diminishes in numbers annually; no doubt in time he will be a kind of pariah. Colleges compete with each other in the Schools. Evening papers prove by statistics the immorality of an establishment where a

GOLF AT OXFORD. THE PLATEAU HOLE AND ARNOLD'S TREE.
Drawn by Lancelot Speed.

scholar who obtains a second is allowed to remain in residence. The stress and strain of the system would be hardly bearable were it not decidedly less difficult to obtain a class in honours than it used to be—not, perhaps, a First, or even a Second; but certainly the lower grades are easier of attainment. Then the variety of subjects is such as to appeal to every one: history, law, theology, natural science (in all its branches), mathematics, all invite the ambitious student whose relations wish him to take honours, and will be quite satisfied with a Fourth; and eminent specialists compete for the privilege of instructing him. The tutor who complained to the undergraduate that he had sixteen pupils was met by the just retort that the undergraduate had sixteen tutors.

The relation of the University to the undergraduate is twofold; it is 'kept'—as a witty scholar of Dublin is fabled to have inscribed over the door of his Dean, 'for his amusement and instruction'—and if the latter is frequently formal, it is still more often and in a great variety of ways 'informal,' and not communicated through his tutor. Not to mention the many college literary societies— every college has one at least, and they are all ready to discuss any topic, from the Origin of Evil to bimetallism—there are now in the University various learned societies, modelled and sometimes called after the German *Seminar*, which are intended to supplement the deficiencies of tuition, and to keep the serious student abreast of the newest erudition which has been 'made in Germany,' or anywhere else on the Continent. Then there is the Union as a school of eloquence for the political aspirant ; or the 'private business' of his college debating society, where a vote of censure on Ministers is sometimes emphasised by their ejection into the quadrangle, may qualify him for the possible methods of a future House of Commons.

III

OF SIGHTSEERS

'The women longed to go and see the college and the tutour.'
'The Guardian's Instruction,' by Stephen Penton.

WHEN the late Mr. Bright asserted that the tone of Oxford life and thought was 'provincial with a difference,' great indignation was aroused in the breasts of all Oxford men — residents, at least ; whether it was the provincialism or the 'difference' wherein lay the sting of the taunt. Probably it was the first. For, although it is a tenable hypothesis that *Kleinstädtigkeit* has really been a potent factor in the production of much that is best in art and literature, still nobody likes to be called provincial by those whose business is in the metropolis. Caesar said that he would rather be a great man at Gabii, or whatever was the Little Pedlington of Italy, than an ordinary person at Rome ;

but the modern Little Pedlingtonian would seldom confess to so grovelling an ambition, whatever might be his real feelings. He would much sooner be one of the crowd in London than mayor of his native city: so at least he says. And so he is very angry if you call him provincial, and venture to insinuate that his views of life are limited by the jurisdiction of his Local Board or City Council; and thus the University of Oxford refused for a long time to forgive John Bright, and did not quite forget his strictures even when it gave him an honorary degree and called him 'patriae et libertatis amantissimus.' And yet the authorities had done what they could to keep the University provincial. It was only after many and deep searchings of heart that the Hebdomadal Council consented to countenance the advent of the Great Western Railway; while the ten miles which separate Oxford from Steventon preserved undergraduates from the contaminating contact of the metropolis there was still hope, but many venerable Tories held that University discipline was past praying for when a three-hours' run would bring you into the heart of the dissipation of London. Some there were who could not even imagine that so terrible a change had really taken place; it is said that Dr. Routh, the President of Magdalen, who attained the respectable age of ninety-nine in the year 1855 (he was elected towards the close of the last century as a *warming-pan*, being then of a delicate constitution and not supposed likely to live!), persistently ignored the development of railways altogether; when undergraduates came up late at the beginning of the winter term, he would excuse them on the ground of the badness of the roads.

We have changed all that, like other provincial centres; and undergraduates who want to 'see their dentist'—a venerable and time-honoured plea which we have heard expressed by the delicate-minded as 'the necessity for keeping a dental engagement'—may now run up to town and back between lunch and 'hall;' the latter function having also marched with the times, and even six-o'clock dinner being now almost a thing of the past. Not so long ago five was the regular hour. In the early seventies seven-o'clock dinner was regarded as a doubtful innovation; and there we have stopped for the present. But the fashionable world outside the colleges imitates London customs—always keeping a little way behind the age—and what has been called the 'Parks System' actually dines as late as 7.45 when it is determined to be *très chic*. It is only one sign of the influx of metropolitan ideas; but there are many others. Oxford tradesmen have learnt by bitter experience that the modern undergraduate is not an exclusive preserve for them like his father. That respected county magnate, when he was at Oriel, bought his coats from an Oxford tailor and his wine from an Oxford wine-merchant, to whom — being an honest man — he paid about half as much again as he would have paid anywhere in London, thereby recouping the men of coats or of wines for the many

COMMEMORATION: OUTSIDE THE SHELDONIAN THEATRE.
Drawn by T. H. Crawford.

bad debts made by dealing with the transitory and impecunious undergraduate. But his son gets his clothes in London, and his wine from the college, which deals directly with Bordeaux. And the tone and subject of conversation is changed too. Oxford is thoroughly up to date, and knows all about the latest play at the Criterion and the latest scandal in the inner circle of London society — or thinks it does, at any rate: there is no one who knows so much about London as the man who does not live there.

But if Oxford goes to London, so does London come to Oxford. Whether it be fitting or not that the site of a theoretically learned University should be in summer a sort of people's park or recreation-ground for the jaded Londoner, the fact is so: the classes and the masses are always with us in one form or another. It has become a common and laudable practice for East-end clergymen and the staff of Toynbee Hall and the Oxford House to bring down their flocks on Whit-Monday or other appropriate

occasions ; and one may constantly see high
academic dignitaries piloting an unwieldy train
of excursionists, and trying to compress Uni-
versity history into a small compass, or to
explain the nature of a college (of all pheno-
mena most unexplainable to the lay mind) to
an audience which has never seen any other
place of education than a Board school. As
for the classes, they have raised the Eights and
'Commem.' to the rank of regular engage-
ments in a London season, and they go through
both with that unflinching heroism which
the English public invariably display in the
performance of a social duty : they shiver in
summer frocks on the barges, despite the hail
and snowstorms of what is ironically described
as the 'Summer' term ; and after a hard day's
sightseeing they enjoy a well-earned repose
by going to Commemoration balls, where you
really do dance, not for a perfunctory two
hours or so, but from 8.30 to 6.30 a.m. In
spite of these hardships it is gratifying to ob-
serve that, whether or not the University suc-
ceeds in its educational mission, it appears to

IN COLLEGE ROOMS.
Drawn by T. H. Crawford.

leave nothing to be desired as a place of amusement for the jaded pleasure-seeker. People who go to sleep at a farce have been known to smile at the (to a resident) dullest and least impressive University function. Ladies appear to take an especial delight in penetrating the mysteries of College life. Perhaps the female mind is piqued by a subdued flavour of impropriety, dating from a period when colleges were not what they are; or more probably they find it gratifying to the self-respect of a superior sex to observe and to pity the notoriously ineffectual attempts of mere bachelors to render existence bearable. So much for the term; and when the vacation begins Oxford is generally inundated by a swarm of heterogeneous tourists—Americans, who come here on their way between Paris and Stratford-on-Avon; Germans, distinguished by a white umbrella and a red 'Baedeker,' trying to realise that here, too, is a University, despite the absence of students with slashed noses and the altogether different quality of the beer. Then with

August come the Extension students; the more frivolous to picnic at Nuneham and Islip, the seriously-minded to attend lectures which compress all knowledge into a fortnight's course, and to speculate on the future when they—the real University, as they say—will succeed to the inheritance of an unenlightened generation which is wasting its great opportunities.

At Commemoration a general sense of lobster salad pervades the atmosphere, and the natural beauties of colleges are concealed or enhanced by a profusion of planking and red cloth; the architectural merit of a hall is as nothing compared to the elasticity of its floor. The Eights, again, provide attractions of their own, not especially academic. The truly judicious sightseer will avoid both of these festive seasons, and will choose some time when there is less to interfere with his own proper pursuit—the week after the Eights, perhaps, or the beginning of the October term, when the red Virginia creeper makes a pleasing contrast with the grey collegiate

A BALL AT CHRIST CHURCH.
Drawn by T. H. Crawford

walls. Nor will he, if he is wise, allow himself to be 'rushed' through the various objects of interest: there are, it is believed, local guides who profess to show the whole of Oxford in two hours; but rumour asserts that the feat is accomplished by making the several quadrangles of one college do duty for a corresponding number of separate establishments, so that the credulous visitor leaves Christ Church with the impression that he has seen not only 'The House,' but also several other foundations, all curiously enough communicating with each other. And in any case, after a mere scamper through the colleges, nothing remains in the mind but a vague and inaccurate reminiscence, combining in one the characteristics of all; the jaded sightseer goes back to London with a fortunately soon-to-be-forgotten idea that Keble was founded by Alfred the Great, and that Tom Quad is a nickname for the Vice-Chancellor. Samuel Pepys seems to have been to a certain extent the prototype of this kind of curiosity or antiquity hunter, and paid a 'shilling to a boy that showed me the Colleges before dinner.' (Curiously enough, 'after dinner' the honorarium to 'one that showed us the schools and library' was 10*s.*!)

He who is responsible for the proper conduct of a gang of relations or friends will not treat them in this way. He will endeavour, so far as possible, to confine them within the limits of his own college, where he is on his native heath, and, if he is not an antiquarian, can at least animate the venerable buildings with details of contemporary history. He will point out his Dons (like the great French nation, 'objects of hatred or admiration, but never of indifference') with such derision or reverence as they may deserve, and affix to them ancient anecdotes whereby their personality may be remembered. He will show to an admiring circle the statue which was painted green, the pinnacle climbed by a friend in the confidence of inebriation, and the marks of the bonfire which the Dean did not succeed in putting out. Even the most ignorant and frivolous-minded person can make his own college interesting. When he has succeeded in impressing upon his friends the true character of a college as a place of religion and sound learning, he may be permitted to show them such external objects as form a part of every one's education, and which no one (for the very shame of confessing it) can pretermit unseen, such as the gardens of New College or St. John's, the 'Nose' of B. N. C., the Burne-Jones tapestry at Exeter, or the picture of Mr. Gladstone in the hall of Christ Church. Those who absolutely insist on a more comprehensive view of the University and City may be allowed to make the ascent of some convenient point of view—Magdalen Tower, for instance; it is a stiff climb, but the view from the top will repay your exertions. This is where, as since the appearance of Mr. Holman Hunt's picture everybody is probably aware, the choir of the college annually salute the rising sun from the top of the tower by singing a Latin hymn on May morning—while the youth of the city, for reasons certainly not known to themselves, make morning hideous with blowing of unmelodious horns in the street below. At all times—even at sunrise on a rainy May morning—it is a noble prospect. The unlovely red-brick suburbs of the north are hidden from sight by the intervening towers and pinnacles of the real Oxford; immediately below the High Street winds westwards, flanked by colleges and churches, of which the prevailing grey is relieved by the green trees of those many gardens and unexplored nooks of verdure with which Oxford abounds; to the south there are glimpses of the river flowing towards the dim grey line of the distant Berkshire downs. To the historically-minded the outlook may suggest many a picture of bygone times— scenes of brawling in the noisy High Street, when the old battle of Town and Gown was fought with cold steel, and blood flowed freely on both sides—in the days when the maltreated townsman appealing to the Proctor could get no satisfaction but a 'thrust at him with his poleaxe!' Down the street which lies below passed Queen Elizabeth—'Virgo

THE DEER PARK, MAGDALEN COLLEGE, OXFORD.
By J. H. Lorimer.

Pia Docta Felix'—after being royally entertained with sumptuous pageants and the play of 'Palamon and Arcyte' in the Christ Church hall. Over the Cherwell, in the troublous times of the Civil Wars, rode the Royalist horse to beat up the Parliamentary quarters below the Chiltern hills and among the woods of the Buckinghamshire border—enterprising undergraduates perhaps taking an *exeat* to accompany them. Here it was that certain scholars of Magdalen, having a quarrel with Lord Norreys by reason of deer-stealing, 'went up privately to the top of their tower, and waiting till he should pass by towards Ricot' (Rycote) 'sent down a shower of stones upon him and his retinew, wounding some and endangering others of their lives'—and worse might have happened had not the 'retinew' taken the precaution, foreseeing the assault, to put boards or tables on their heads. At a later day Pope entered Oxford by this road, and there is a pretty description of the scene in one of his letters—it will no doubt appeal to the nineteenth-century visitor who departs through slums to the architecturally unimpressive station of the Great Western. 'The shades of the evening overtook me. The moon rose in the clearest sky I ever saw, by whose solemn light I paced on slowly, without company, or any interruption to the range of my own thoughts. About a mile before I reached Oxford all the bells tolled in different notes, the clocks of every college answered one another, and sounded forth (some in a deeper, some in a softer tone) that it was eleven at night. All this was no ill preparation to the life I have led since among those old walls, venerable galleries, stone porticos, studious walks, and solitary scenes of the University.' Jerry-built rows of lodging-houses rather militate against the romance of the Iffley Road as we know it now.

But, after all, the majority of sightseers are not given to historical reflections. What most people want is something that 'palpitates with actuality;' they want to see the machine working. They are temporarily happy if they can see a Proctor in his robes of office, and

IN CONVOCATION: CONFERRING A DEGREE.
Drawn by Ernest Stamp.

rise to the enthusiasm of 'never having had such a delightful day' if the Proctor happens to 'proctorise' an undergraduate within the ken of their vision. 'It was all so *delightful* and mediaeval, and all that kind of thing, don't you know? Poor young man—simply for not wearing one of those horrid caps and gowns! *I* call it a shame.' This is the reason why a Degree Day is so wonderfully popular a ceremony. There is a sense of attractive mystery about it all—the Vice-Chancellor throned in the Theatre or Convocation House, discoursing in unintelligible scraps of Latin like the refrain of a song, and the Proctors doing their quarter-deck walk—although the dignity of the function be rather marred by the undergraduates who jostle and giggle in the background forgetting that they are assisting at a ceremony which is, after all, one of the University's reasons of existence. It is the same kind of curiosity which causes the lecturer to become suddenly conscious that he is being watched with intense interest—an interest to which he is altogether unaccustomed—by 'only a face at the window' of his lecture-room, to his own confusion and the undisguised amusement of his audience.

Such are sightseers: yet every man to his taste. When Samuel Pepys came over from Abingdon to see the sights of the University town, it is gratifying and rather surprising to learn that what most impressed him was the small price paid for creature comforts : 'Oxford mighty fine place,' such is the diarist's reflection, 'and *cheap entertainment.*'

IV

OF EXAMINATIONS

'Thinketh one made them in a fit of the blues.'

Q.

IF there is one subject on which the professedly non-reading undergraduate is nearly always eloquent it is the aggravation of his naturally hard lot by the examination system; that is, not only 'The Schools' themselves, but the ancillary organization of lectures, 'collections,' and college tuition in general; all which machinery, being intended to save him from himself and enable him to accomplish the ostensible purpose of his residence at the University, he very properly regards as an entirely unnecessary instrument of torture, designed and perfected by the gratuitous and malignant ingenuity of Dons, whose sole object is the oppression of undergraduates in general and himself in particular.

He is obliged to attend lectures, at least occasionally. His tutors compel him to attempt to pass his University examination at a definite date ; and then—adding insult to injury— actually reproach him or even send him down for his ill success, just as if he had not always demonstrated to them by repeated statements and constant proofs of incapacity that he had not the smallest intention of getting through! Small wonder, perhaps, that on returning from a highly unsatisfactory interview with the University examiners to a yet more exasperating colloquy with the authorities of his college, he should wish that fate had not matched him with the 'cosmic process' of the nineteenth century; and that it had been his happier lot to come up to Oxford in the days when examinations were not, and his remote ancestors got their degrees without any vain display of mere intellectual proficiency, or went down without them if they chose.

And yet, should the modern undergraduate take the trouble (which of course he never

A LECTURE-ROOM IN MAGDALEN COLLEGE.
Drawn by E. Stamp.

does) to acquaint himself with the statutes and ordinances which governed his University in the pre-examination period, he would find that even then the rose was not wholly devoid of thorns. Even then the powers that be had decreed that life should not be completely beer, nor altogether skittles. It is true that the student was probably less molested by his college; but the regulations of the University dealt far more hardly with him than they do at present. Under the statutes of Archbishop Laud, the University exercised those functions of teaching and general supervision which it has since in great part surrendered to its component colleges; and in theory the University was a hard task-mistress.

Attendance at professorial lectures was theoretically obligatory, and 'since not only reading and thought, but practice also, is of the greatest avail towards proficiency in learning,' it was required that the candidate for a degree should 'dispute' in the Schools at stated and frequent times during the whole course of his academic career. Beginning by listening to the disputations of his seniors (a custom which perhaps survives in the modern fashion which sometimes provides a 'gallery' at the ceremony of *viva voce*), he was as time went on required himself to maintain and publicly defend doctrines in a manner which would be highly embarrassing to his modern successor—'responding' at first to the arguments of the stater of a theory, and with riper wisdom being promoted to the position of 'opponent.' This opposing and responding was termed 'doing generals.' 'Argufying' was the business of the University in the seventeenth century, and had been so for a long time.

On the memorable occasion of Queen Elizabeth's visit to Oxford in the year 1566, Her Majesty was entertained intermittently with disputations on the moon's influence on the tides, and the right of rebellion against bad government. Thus, 'Archbishop Laud required of the seventeenth-century undergraduate so many disputations before he became a *sophista*, and so many again before he could be admitted to the degree of Bachelor; and if the system had worked in practice as it was intended to do in theory, young Oxford would not have had an easy time of it. In the days of Antony Wood's undergraduate career exercises in the 'Schooles' were 'very good.' ' Philosophy disputations in Lent time, frequent in the Greek tongue; *coursing* very much, ending alwaies in blowes,' which Wood considers scandalous; but at least it shows the serious spirit of the disputants. But a University can always be trusted to temper the biting wind of oppressive regulations to its shorn alumni; and there can be no doubt that the comparative slackness and sleepiness of the eighteenth century — a somnolence which it is easy to exaggerate, but impossible altogether to deny — must have tended to wear the sharp corners off the academic curriculum. Indications that this was so are not wanting. After all, there must have been many ways of avoiding originality in a disputation. A writer in 'Terrae Filius' (1720) states the case as follows :—

'All students in the University who are above one year's standing, and have not taken their batchelor' (of arts) 'degree, are required by statute to be present at this awful solemnity' (disputation for a degree), 'which is design'd for a public proof of the progress he has made in the art of reasoning; tho' in fact it is no more than a formal repetition of a set of syllogisms upon some ridiculous question in logick, which they get by rote, or, perhaps, only read out of their caps, which lie before them with their notes in them. These commodious sets of syllogisms are call'd strings, and descend from undergraduate to undergraduate, in regular succession; so that, when any candidate for a degree is to exercise his talent in argumentation, he has nothing else to do but to enquire amongst his friends for a string upon such-and-such a question.'

So, even in the early part of the present century, reverend persons proceeding to the degree of D.D. have been known to avail themselves of a thesis (or written harangue on some point of theology) not compiled by their unaided exertions, but kept among the archives of their college and passed round as occasion might require. If mature theologians have reconciled this with their consciences in the nineteenth, what may not have been possible to an undergraduate in the eighteenth century? Also, the functionary who stood in the place of the modern examiner was a very different kind of person from his successor—that incarnation of cold and impassive criticism; collusion between 'opponent' and 'respondent' must have been possible and frequent; and so far had things gone that the candidate for a degree was permitted to choose the 'Master' who was to examine him, and it appears to have been customary to invite your Master to dinner on the night preceding the final disputation. Witness 'Terrae Filius' once more :—

'Most candidates get leave . . . . to chuse their own examiners, who never fail to be their old cronies and toping companions . . . . It is also well known to be the custom for the candidates either to present their examiners with a piece of gold, or to give them a handsome entertainment, and make them drunk, which they commonly do the night before examination, and some times keep them till morning, and so adjourn, cheek by jowl, from their drinking-room to the school, where they are to be examined.'

The same author adds: 'This to me seems the great business of *determination:* to pay money and get drunk.'

Vicesimus Knox, who took his B.A. degree in 1775, is at pains to represent the whole process of so-called examination as an elaborate farce. 'Every candidate,' he says, 'is obliged to be examined in the whole circle of the sciences by three masters of arts, of his own choice.' Naturally, the temptation is too much for poor humanity. 'It is reckoned good management to get acquainted with two or three jolly young masters and supply them well with port previously to the examination.' *Viva voce* once put on this convivial footing, it is not surprising that 'the examiners and the candidate often converse on the last drinking bout, or on horses, or read the newspapers, or a novel, or divert themselves as well as they can till the clock strikes eleven, when all parties descend, and the *testimonium* is signed by the masters.' Under such circumstances it is obvious that the provisions of Archbishop Laud might be shorn of half their terrors. Even at an earlier period other methods of evasion were not wanting. As early as 1656, orders were made 'abolishing' the custom of candidates standing treat to examiners. In the statute which still prescribes the duties of the *clericus universitatis*, there is a clause threatening him with severe penalties—to the extent of paying a fine of ten shillings—should he so far misuse his especial charge, the University clock, as to 'retard and presently precipitate the course' of that venerable timepiece, 'in such a manner that the hours appointed for public exercises be unjustly shortened, to the harm and prejudice of the studious.' Moreover, we read in Wood that notice of examination was given by 'tickets stuck up on certaine public corners, which would be suddenly after taken downe' by the candidate's friends. To such straits and to such unworthy shifts could disputants be reduced by mere inability to find matter.

It has been said that attendance at professorial lectures was theoretically obligatory; but it is hardly necessary to point out that even serious students have occasionally dispensed with the duty of attending lectures; and it is more than whispered there have been occasions in recent centuries when it was not an audience only that was wanting. There are, of course, instances of both extremes. Rumour tells of a certain professor of anatomy, who, lacking a quorum, bade his servant 'bring out the skeleton, in order that I may be able to address you as "gentle*men*;"' but all professors have not been so conscientious. Gibbon goes so far as to assert that 'in the University of Oxford, the greater part of the public professors have for these many years given up altogether the pretence of teaching,' and the Reverend James Hurdie does not much improve the matter, when he prepares to refute the historian's charge in his 'Vindication of Magdalen College.' So far as the College is concerned, the reverend gentleman has something of a case; but his defence of the University is not altogether satisfying. Some of the professors, no doubt, do lecture in a statutable manner. But 'the late noble but unfortunate Professor of Civil Law began his office with reading lectures, and only desisted for want of an audience' (a plausible excuse, were it not that some lecturers seem to have entertained peculiar ideas as to the constitution of an audience. 'Terrae Filius' has a story of a Professor of Divinity who came to his lecture-room, found to his surprise and displeasure, a band of intending hearers, and dismissed them straightway with the summary remark: 'Domini, vos non estis idonei auditores!' 'The present Professor, newly appointed (the author has heard it from the highest authority), means to read.' Moreover, 'the late Professor of Botany at one time *did* read.' In fact, as the 'Oxford Spy' observes in 1818:—

> 'Yet here the rays of Modern Science spread :
> Professors are appointed, lectures read.
> If none attend, or hear : not ours the blame,
> Theirs is the folly — and be theirs the shame.'

It is evident that professorial lectures were not a wholly unbearable burden.

'It is recorded in the veracious chronicle of Herodotus that Sandoces, a Persian judge, had been crucified by Darius, on the charge of taking a bribe to determine a cause wrongly; but while he yet hung on the cross, Darius found by calculation that the good deeds of Sandoces towards the king's house were more numerous than his evil deeds, and so, confessing that he had acted with more haste than wisdom, he ordered him to be taken down and set at large.'

So when the Universities are at last confronted with that great Day of Reckoning which is continually held over their heads by external enemies, and which timorous friends are always trying to stave off by grudging concessions and half-hearted sympathy with Movements; when we are brought to the bar of that grand and final commission, which is once for all to purge Oxford and Cambridge of their last remnants of mediaevalism, and bring them into line with the marching columns

THE LIBRARY, MERTON COLLEGE.
Drawn by Ernest Stamp.

Of Examinations

of modern Democracy; when the judgment is set and the books are opened, we may hope that some extenuating circumstances may be found to set against the long enumeration of academic crimes. There will be no denying that Oxford has been the home of dead languages and undying prejudice. It will be admitted as only too true that Natural Science students were for many years compelled to learn a little Greek, and that colleges have not been prepared to sacrifice the greater part of their immoral revenues to the furtherance of University Extension; and we shall have to plead guilty to the damning charge of having returned two Tory members to several successive Parliaments. All this Oxford has done, and more; there is no getting out of it. Yet her counsel will be able to plead in her favour that once at least she has been found not retarding the rear, but actually leading the van of nineteenth-century progress; for it will hardly be denied that if the Universities did not invent the Examination System, at least they were among the first to welcome and to adapt it ; and that if it had not been for the development of examinations, qualifying and competitive, at Oxford and Cambridge, the ranks of the Civil Service would have continued for many years longer to be recruited by the bad old method of nomination (commonly called jobbery and nepotism by the excluded), and society would, perhaps, never have realised that a knowledge of Chaucer is among the most desirable qualifications for an officer in Her Majesty's Army. Here, at least, the Universities have been privileged to set an example.

The Oxford examination system is practically contemporaneous with the century ; the first regular class list having been published in 1807. The change was long in coming, and when it did come the face of the University was not revolutionised ; if the alteration contained, as it undoubtedly did, the germs of a revolution which was to extend far beyond academic boundaries, it bore the aspect of a most desirable but most moderate reform. Instead of obtaining a degree by the obsolete process of perfunctory disputation, ambitious men were invited to offer certain books (classical works for the most part), and in these to undergo the ordeal of a written and oral examination ; the oral part being at that time probably as important as the other. Sudden and violent changes are repugnant to all Englishmen, and more especially to the rulers of Universities, those homes of ancient tradition ; and just as early railways found it difficult to escape from the form of the stage-coach and the old nomenclature of the road, so the new Final Honour School took over (so to speak) the plant of a system which it superseded. *Viva voce* was still (and is to the present day) important, because it was the direct successor of oral disputation. The candidate for a degree had obtained that distinction by a theoretical argument with three 'opponents' in the Schools ; so now the opponents were represented by a nearly corresponding number of examiners, and the *viva voce* part of the examination was for a long time regarded as a contest of wit between the candidate and the questioner. Nor did the race for honours affect the great majority of the University as it does at present. It was intended for the talented few : it was not a matter of course that Tom, Dick, and Harry should go in for honours because their friends wished it, or because their college tutor wished to keep his college out of the evening papers. Candidates for honours were regarded as rather exceptional persons, and a brilliant performance in the Schools was regarded as a tolerably sure augury of success in life : a belief which was, perhaps, justified by facts then, but which—like most beliefs, dying hard — has unfortunately survived into a state of society where it is impossible to provide the assurance of a successful career for all and each of the eighty or hundred 'first-class' men whom the University annually presents to an unwelcoming world.

However small its beginnings it was inevitable that the recognition of intellect should exercise the greatest influence — though not immediately and obviously—on the future of

READING THE NEWDIGATE.

Drawn by T. H. Crawford.

Of Examinations

the University. *La carrière* once *ouverte aux talents*—the fact being established and recognised that one man was intellectually not only as good as another, but a deal better—colleges could not help following the example set them; the first stirrings of 'inter-collegiate competition' began to be felt, and after forty years or so (for colleges generally proceed in these and similar matters with commendable caution, and it was only the earlier part of the nineteenth century after all) began the gradual abolition of 'close' scholarships and fellowships — those admirable endowments whereby the native of some specified county or town was provided with a competence for life, solely in virtue of the happy accident of birth. To disregard talent openly placarded and certificated was no longer possible. The most steady-going and venerable institutions began to be reanimated by the infusion of new blood, and to be pervaded by the newest and most 'dangerous' ideas.

Nor were the outside public slow to avail themselves after their manner of the changed state of things. The possessor of a University degree has at all times been regarded by less fortunate persons with a kind of superstitious awe, as one who has lived in mysterious precincts and practised curious (if not always useful) arts, and at first the title of 'Honourman,' implying that the holder belonged to a privileged few—*élite* of the *élites*—whom a University, itself learned, had delighted to honour for their learning, could inspire nothing less than reverence. Also the distinction was a very convenient one. The public is naturally only too glad to have any ready and satisfactory testimonial which may help as a method of selection among the host of applicants for its various employments; and here was a diploma signed by competent authorities and bearing no suspicion of fear or favour. Presently the public began to follow the lead of Oxford and Cambridge, and examine for itself, but that is another story: schoolmasters more especially have always kept a keen eye on the class list. So an intellectual distinction comes in time to have a commercial price, and this no doubt has had something (though, we will hope, not everything) to do with the increase in the number of 'Schools' and the growing facilities for obtaining so-called honours. But it is needless to observe that the multiplication of the article tends to the depreciation of its value. The First-class man, who was a potential Cabinet Minister or an embryo Archbishop at the beginning of the century, is now capable of descending to all kinds of employments. He does not indeed— being perhaps conscious of incapacity—serve as a waiter in a hotel, after the fashion of American students in the vacation, but he has been known to accept gratefully a post in a private school where his tenure of office depends largely on the form he shows in bowling to the second eleven.

Here in Oxford, though we still respect a 'First,' and though perhaps the greater part of our available educational capacity is devoted to the conversion of passmen into honourmen, there are signs that examinations are no longer quite regarded as the highest good and the chief object of existence. It is an age of specialism, and yet it is hard to mould the whole University system to suit the particular studies of every specialist. Multiply Final Schools as you will, 'the genuine student' with one engrossing interest will multiply far more quickly; and just as the athlete and non-reading man complains that the schools interrupt his amusements, the man who specialises on the pips of an orange, or who regards nothing in history worth reading except a period of two years and six months in the later Byzantine empire, will pathetically lament that examinations are interrupting his real work. Are men made for the Schools, or the Schools for men? It is a continual problem; perhaps examinations are only a *pis aller*, and we must be content to wait till science instructs us how to gauge mental faculty by experiment without subjecting the philosopher to the ordeal of Latin Prose, and the 'pure scholar' to the test of a possibly useless acquaintance with the true inwardness of Hegelianism. After all it is the greatest happiness of the greatest number that has to be considered, and the majority as yet are not special students. Moreover, there are various kinds of specialists. If 'general knowledge' (as has been said) is too often synonymous with 'particular ignorance,' it is equally true that specialism in one branch is sometimes not wholly unconnected with failure in another.

It was the severance of another link with the past when the scene of examinations was transferred from the 'Old Schools'—the purlieus of the Sheldonian and the Bodleian—to a new and perhaps unnecessarily palatial building in the High Street, which is as little in keeping with the dark, crumbling walls of its neighbour, University College, as the motley throng of examinees (*pueri innuptaeque puellae*) is out of harmony with the traditions of an age which did not recognise the necessity of female education. We have changed all that, and possibly the change is for the better, for while the atmosphere which pervaded the ancient dens now appropriated to the use of the great library was certainly academic, and was sometimes cool and pleasant in summer, the conditions of the game became almost intolerable in winter. Unless he would die under the process of examinations like the Chinese of story, the candidate must provide himself with greatcoats and rugs enough (it was said) to hide a 'crib,' or even a Liddell and Scott, for the proximity of the Bodleian forbade any lighting or warming apparatus. But in the new examination schools comfort and luxury reign; rare marbles adorn even the least conspicuous corners, and the only survivals of antiquity are the ancient tables, which are popularly supposed to be contemporaneous with the examination system, and are bescrawled and bescratched with every possible variety of inscription and hieroglyphic — from adaptations of verses in the Psalms to a list of possible Derby winners—from a caricature of the 'invigilating' examiner to a sentimental but unflattering reminiscence of one's partner at last night's dance. Here they sit, a remarkable medley, all sorts, conditions, and even ages of men, herded together as they probably never will

A DANCE AT ST. JOHN'S.
Drawn by T. Hamilton Crawford, R.W.S.

be again in after-life : undeserving talent cheek by jowl with meritorious dulness; callow youth fresh from the rod of the schoolmaster, and mature age with a family waiting anxiously outside; and a minority of the fairer sex, whose presence is rather embarrassing to examiners who do not see their way to dealing with possible hysteria. And in the evening they will return—if it is Commemoration week; the venerable tables will be cleared away, and the 'Scholae Magnae Borealis et Australis' will be used for the more desirable purpose of dancing. Is it merely soft nothings that the Christ Church undergraduate is whispering to that young lady from Somerville Hall, as they 'sit out' the lancers in the romantic light of several hundred Chinese lanterns? Not at all; they are comparing notes about their *viva voce* in history.

V

UNIVERSITY JOURNALISM

> 'I only wish my critics had to write
> A High-class Paper!'
> *Anon.*

THE business of those who teach in the Universities is to criticise mistakes, and criticism of style has two results for the master and the scholar. It may produce that straining after correctness in small matters which the cold world calls pedantry; and in the case of those who are not content only to observe, but are afflicted with a desire to produce, criticism of style takes the form of parody or imitation; for a good parody or a good imitation of an author's manner is an object-lesson in criticism. Hence it is that that same intolerance of error which makes members of a University slow in the production of really great works stimulates the genesis of ephemeral and mostly imitative literature. The more Oxford concerns herself with literary style, the more she is likely in her less serious moods to ape the manner of contemporary literature. It all comes, in the first instance, of being taught to copy Sophocles and travesty Virgil. Ephemeral literature, then, at the Universities has always been essentially imitative. In the last century, when it was the fashion to be classical—and when as in the earlier poems of Mr. Barry Lyndon, 'Sol bedecked the verdant mead, or pallid Luna shed her ray'— Oxonian minor poets imitated the London wits and sang the charms of the local belles under the sobriquets of Chloe and Delia, and academic essayists copied the manner of the 'Spectator,' and hit off the weaknesses of their friends, Androtion and Clearchus; and now that the world has come to be ruled by newspapers, it is only natural that the style and the methods of the daily and weekly press should in some degree affect the lighter literature of Universities, and that not only undergraduates, who are naturally imitative, but even dons, who might be supposed to know better, should find themselves contributing to and redacting publications which are conducted more or less on the lines of the 'new journalism.'

Oxford has been slow to develop in this particular direction, and the reasons are not far to seek. The conditions just now are exceptionally favourable — that is, a *cacoëthes scribendi* has coincided with abundance of matter to write about, but the organs of the great external world naturally provide a model for the writer. But it is only recently that these causes have been all together present and operative, and the absence of one or more of them has at different times been as effectual as the absence of all. In the early part of the present century there can have been no lack of matter : University reform was at least in the air, athletics were developing, the examination system was already in full swing. But for some reason the tendency of the University was not in the direction of the production of ephemeral or at least frivolous literature. The pompous Toryism of Uni-

THE RADCLIFFE.
Drawn by Ernest Stamp.

versity authorities seventy years ago did not encourage any intellectual activity unconnected with the regular curriculum of the student, and when intellectual activity began to develop, it was rather on the lines of theological discussion — the subjects were hardly fitted for the columns of a newspaper. At an earlier date the Vice-Chancellor was interviewed by the delegate of an aspiring clique of undergraduates, who wished to form a literary club and to obtain the sanction of authority for its formation. He refused to grant the society any formal recognition, on the ground that while it was true that the statutes did not absolutely forbid such things, they certainly did not specifically mention them; and the members of the club—when it was eventually founded independent of the Vice-Cancellarial auspices—were known among their friends as the 'Lunatics.' Such was the somewhat obscurantist temper of the University about the year 1820; and we can imagine that the Vice-Chancellor, who could find nothing in the statutes encouraging a debating society, would not have looked with enthusiastic approbation on a newspaper designed to discuss University matters without respect for authority. Even if he had, it would have been hard to appeal to all sections of the community; though there was certainly more general activity in the University than formerly, the *gaudia* and *discursus* of undergraduates were matters of comparatively small importance to their friends, and of none at all to their pastors and masters.

In the earlier part of the eighteenth century the conditions were exactly reversed. To judge from the specimens that have survived to the present day (and how much of our own lighter literature will be in evidence 170 years hence?) there must have been plenty of 'available talent.' It was an age of essayists. Addison and Steele set the fashion for the metropolis: and as has been said before, Oxford satirists followed at some distance in the wake of these giants. The form of 'Terrae Filius' is that of the 'Tatler' and 'Spectator,' and the 'Oxford Magazine' of that day is largely composed of essays on men, women, and manners; many are still quite readable, and most have been recognised as remarkably smart in their day. Nor is it only in professed and formal satire that the talent of the time displays itself. Thomas Hearne of the Bodleian was careful to keep a voluminous note-book, chronicling not only the 'plums' extracted by his daily researches from the dark recesses of the library, but also various anecdotes, scandalous or respectable, of his contemporaries; and one is tempted to regret that so admirable a talent for bepraising his friends and libelling his enemies should be comparatively *perdu* among extracts from 'Schoppius de Arte Critica,' copies of church brasses, and such-like antiquarian lumber —the whole forming a 'Collection' only recently published for the world's edification by the Oxford Historical Society. His 'appreciations' would have made the fortune of any paper relying for its main interest on personalities, after the fashion which we are learning from the Americans. Descriptions of his friends and enemies, such as 'An extravagant, haughty, loose man,' 'a Dull, Stupid, whiggish Companion,' are frequent and free; and anecdotes of obscure college scandal abound. We read how the 'Snivelling, conceited, and ignorant, as well as Fanatical Vice-Principal of St. Edmund Hall . . . . *sconc'd* two gentlemen, which is a Plain Indication of his Furious Temper;' and how 'Mr. —— of *Christ Church* last *Easter-day*, under pretence of being ill, desired one of the other chaplains to read Prayers for him: which accordingly was done. Yet such was the impudence of the man that he appeared in the Hall at dinner!'

As it was, however, those very collections which exhibit Hearne's peculiar genius show us at the same time how impossible, even granting the supposition to be not altogether anachronistic, a regular University 'News-letter' would have been. We talk now in a vague and, perhaps, rather unintelligible fashion of 'University politics,' and in some way contrive to identify Gladstonianism with a susceptibility to the claims of a school of English literature, or whatever is the latest phrase of progress—mixing up internal legislation with the external

IN THE BODLEIAN.

Drawn by Ernest Stamp.

politics of the great world. But in Hearne's time there were no University politics to discuss. 'Their toasts,' says Gibbon of the Fellows of Magdalen College, 'were not expressive of the most lively loyalty to the House of Hanover,' and Hearne's interest in politics has nothing to do with the Hebdomadal Council. When he speaks of 'our white-liver'd Professor, Dr. ———,' or describes the highest official in the University as 'old Smooth-boots, the Vice-Chancellor,' it is generally for the very sufficient reason that the person in question is what Dr. Johnson called a 'vile Whig.' But Tory politics and common-room scandal and jobbery apart, the University would appear to have slept the sleep of the unjust. 'Terrae Filius' grumbles at the corrupt method of 'examination,' and 'The Student' is lively and satirical on the peccadilloes and escapades of various members of society. But your prose essayist is apt to be intermittent, and the publication that relies mainly on him leans on a breaking reed; so that we can hardly be surprised that the last-named periodical should eke out its pages with imitations of Tibullus, to the first of which the Editor appends the encouraging note, 'If this is approved by the publick, the Author will occasionally oblige us with more *Elegies* in the same style and manner.'

Now that every one is anxious to see his own name and his friend's name in print, and that the general public takes, or pretends to take, a keen interest in the details of every cricket-match and boat-race, a paper chronicling University matters cannot complain of the smallness of its *clientèle*. Every one wants news. The undergraduate who has made a speech at the Union, or a century for his college second eleven, wants a printed certificate of his glorious achievements. Dons, and undergraduates too, for that matter, are anxious to read about the last hint of a possible Commission or the newest thing in University Extension. Men who have gone down but a short time ago are still interested in the doings of the (of course degenerate) remnant who are left; and even the non-academic Oxford residents, a large and increasing class, are on the watch for some glimpse of University doings, and some distant echo of common-room gossip. Modern journalism appeals more or less to all these classes; it cannot complain of the want of an audience, nor, on the whole, of a want of news to satisfy it, and certainly an Oxford organ cannot lack models for imitation, or awful examples to avoid. It is, in fact, the very multiplicity of contemporary periodicals that is the source of difficulty. A paper conducted in the provinces by amateurs—that is, by persons who have also other things to do—is always on its probation. The fierce light of the opinion of a limited public is continually beating on it. Its contributors should do everything a little better than the hirelings of the merely professional organs of the unlearned metropolis; its leaders must be more judicious than those of the 'Times,' its occasional notes a little more spicy than Mr. Labouchere's, and its reviews a little more learned than those of the 'Journal of Philology.' Should it fall short of perfection in any of these branches, it 'has no reason for existence,' and is in fact described as 'probably moribund.' Yet another terror is added to the life of an Oxford editor: he *must* be at least often 'funny;' he must endeavour in some sort to carry out the great traditions of the 'Oxford Spectator' and the 'Shotover Papers;' and as the English public is generally best amused by personalities, he must be careful to observe the almost invisible line which separates the justifiable skit from the offensive attack. Now, the undergraduate contributor to the press is seldom successful as a humourist. He is occasionally violent and he is often — more especially after the festive season of Christmas—addicted to sentimental verse; but for mere frivolity and 'lightness of touch' it is safer to apply to his tutor.

It is a rather remarkable fact that almost all University papers—certainly all that have succeeded under the trying conditions of the game—have been managed and for the most part written, not by the exuberant vitality of undergraduate youth, but by the less interesting prudence of graduate maturity. It is remarkable, but not surprising. Undergraduate talent is occasionally brilliant, but is naturally transient. Generations succeed each other with such rapidity that the most capable editorial staff is vanishing into thin air just at the moment when a journal has reached the highest pitch of popularity. Moreover, amateur talent is always hard to deal with, as organizers of private theatricals know to their cost; and there is no member of society more capable of disappointing his friends at a critical moment than the amateur contributor to the press. Should the spirit move him, he will send four columns when the editor wants one; but if he is not in the vein, or happens to have something else to do, there is no promise so sacred and no threat so terrible as to persuade him to put pen to paper. If these are statements of general application, they are doubly true of undergraduates, who are always distracted by a too great diversity of occupations: Jones, whose power of intermittent satire has made him the terror of his Dons, has unaccountably taken to reading for the Schools;

the poet, Smith, has gone into training for the Torpids; and Brown, whose '*Voces Populi* in a Ladies' College' were to have been something quite too excruciatingly funny, has fallen in love in the vacation and will write nothing but bad poetry. Such are the trials of the editor who drives an undergraduate team ; and hence it comes about that the steady-going periodicals for which the public can pay a yearly subscription in advance, with the prospect of seeing at any rate half the value of its money, are principally controlled by graduates. No doubt they sometimes preserve a certain appearance of youthful vigour by worshipping undergraduate talent, and using the word 'Donnish' as often and as contemptuously as possible.

Nevertheless, there appear from time to time various ephemeral and meteoric publications, edited by junior members of the University. They waste the editor's valuable time, no doubt ; and yet he is learning a lesson which may, perhaps, be useful to him in afterlife ; for it is said that until he is undeceived

SAILING ON THE UPPER RIVER. *Drawn by L. Speed.*

by hard experience, every man is born with the conviction that he can do three things—drive a dog-cart, sail a boat, and edit a paper.

VI

THE UNIVERSITY AS SEEN FROM OUTSIDE

> 'A man must serve his time to every trade
> Save censure—critics all are ready made.'
> *Byron.*

IT has been said that the function of a University is to criticise ; but the proposition is at least equally true that Oxford and Cambridge are continually conjugating the verb in the passive. We—and more especially we who live in Oxford, for the sister University apparently is either more virtuous or more skilful in concealing her peccadilloes from the public eye—enjoy the priceless advantage of possessing innumerable friends whose good nature is equalled by their frankness ; and if we do not learn wisdom, that is not because the opportunity is not offered to us. It is true that our great governing body, the Hebdomadal Council, has hitherto preserved its independence by a prudent concealment of its deliberations : no reporter has ever as yet penetrated into that august assemblage ; but whatever emerges to the light of day is seized upon with avidity. Debates in Convocation or even in Congregation (the latter body including only the resident Masters of Arts), although the subject may have been somewhat remote from the interests of the general public, and the number of the voters perhaps considerably increased by the frivolous reason that it was a wet afternoon, when there was nothing else to do than to govern the University—debates on every conceivable subject blush to find themselves reported the next morning almost in the greatest of daily papers ; and perhaps the result of a division on the addition of one more Oriental language to Responsions, or one more crocket to a new pinnacle of St. Mary's Church, is even honoured by a leading article. This is highly gratifying to residents in the precincts of the University, but even to them it is now and then not altogether comprehensible. Nor is

it only questions concerning the University as
a whole which appeal to the external public;
even college business and college scandal some-
times assume an unnatural importance. Years
ago one of the tutors of a certain college was
subjected to the venerable and now almost
obsolete process of 'screwing up,' and some
young gentlemen were rusticated for complicity
in the offence. Even in academic circles the
crime and its punishment were not supposed
to be likely to interfere with the customary
revolution of the solar system; but the editor
of a London daily paper—and one, too, which
was supposed to be more especially in touch
with that great heart of the people which
is well known to hold Universities in con-
tempt—considered the incident so important
as to publish a leading article with the
remarkable exordium, 'Every one knew
that Mr. ——, of —— College, would be
screwed up some day!' Most of the *abonnés*
of this journal must, it is to be feared, have
blushed for their discreditable ignorance of
Mr. ——'s existence, not to mention that

PORCH OF ST. MARY'S.
Drawn by J. Pennell.

leaden-footed retribution which was dogging him to a merited doom.

It is hardly necessary to say that in nine cases out of ten comment on the proceedings of a learned University takes the form of censure: nor are censors far to seek. There are always plenty of young men more or less connected with the Press who have wrongs to avenge; who are only too glad to have an opportunity of 'scoring off' the college authority which did its best —perhaps unsuccessfully, but still with a manifest intention—to embitter their academic existence; or of branding once for all as reactionary and obscurantist the hidebound regulations of a University which did not accord them the highest honours. In these cases accuracy of facts and statistics is seldom a matter of much importance. Generally speaking, you can say what you like about a college, or the University, without much fear of contradiction—provided that you abstain from mere personalities. For one thing, the cap is always fitted on some one else's head. It is not the business of St. Botolph's to concern itself with an attack which is obviously meant for St. Boniface: it is darkly whispered in the St. Boniface common-room that after all no one knows what actually *does* go on in St. Botolph's : and obviously neither of these venerable foundations can have anything to do with answering impeachments of the University and its financial system. Moreover, even if the Dons should rouse themselves from their usual torpor and attempt a defence, it is not very likely that the public will listen to them : any statement proceeding from an academic source being always regarded with the gravest suspicion. That is why 'any stick is good enough to beat the Universities,' and there are always plenty of sticks who are quite ready to perform the necessary castigation.

Moreover, these writers generally deal with a subject which is always interesting, because it is one on which every one has an opinion, and an opinion which is entitled to

The University as seen from Outside

respect—the education of youth. Any one can pick holes in the University system of teaching and examination—'can strike a finger on the place, and say, "Thou ailest here and here,"'—or construct schemes of reform: more especially young men who have recently quitted their Alma Mater, and are therefore qualified to assert (as they do, and at times not without a certain plausibility) that she has failed to teach them anything.

That the British public, with so much to think about, should find time to be diverted by abuse of its seats of learning, is at first a little surprising; but there is no doubt that such satire has an agreeable piquancy, and for tolerably obvious reasons. English humour is generally of the personal kind, and needs a butt; a capacity in which all persons connected with education have from time immemorial been qualified to perform, *ex officio* (education being generally considered as an imparting of unnecessary and even harmful knowledge, and obviously dissociated from the pursuit of financial prosperity, both as regards the teachers and the taught): Shakespeare set the fashion, and Dickens and Thackeray have settled the hash of schoolmasters and college tutors for the next fifty years, at any rate. Schoolmasters, indeed, are becoming so important and prosperous a part of the community that they will probably be the first to reinstate themselves in the respect of the public; but Dons have more difficulties to contend against. They have seldom any prospect of opulence. Then, again, they suffer from the quasi-monastic character of colleges; they have inherited some of the railing accusations which used to be brought against monasteries. The voice of scandal — especially feminine scandal — is not likely to be long silent about celibate societies, and no Rudyard Kipling has yet arisen to plead on behalf of Fellows that they

> 'aren't no blackguards too,
> But single men in barracks, most remarkable like you.'

Altogether the legend of 'monks,' 'port wine and prejudice,' 'dull and deep potations,' and all the rest of it, still damages Dons in the

IN EXETER COLLEGE CHAPEL.
Drawn by E. Stamp.

eyes of the general public. 'That's —— College,' says the local guide to his sightseers, 'and there they sits, on their Turkey carpets, a-drinking of their Madeira, and Burgundy, and Tokay.' Such is, apparently, the impression still entertained by Society. And no doubt successive generations of Fellows who hunted four days a week, or, being in Orders, 'thanked Heaven that no one ever took *them* for parsons,' did to a certain extent perpetuate the traditions of 'Bolton Abbey in the olden time.' Well, their day is over now. If the Fellow *fin de siècle* should ever venture to indulge in the sports of the field, he must pretend that he has met the hounds by accident; and even then he risks his reputation.

It is always pleasant, too, to be wiser than one's erstwhile pastors and masters. The pupil goes out into the great world; the teacher remains behind, and continues apparently to go on in his old and crusted errors. Outwardly the Universities do not change much, and it is easy to assume that the habits and ideas of their denizens do not change either. Thus it is that the young men of the 'National Observer,' coming back from a Saturday-to-Monday visit to a university which they never respected and are now entitled to despise, are moved to declare to the world the complete inutility of what they call the Futile Don. 'He is dead,' they say, 'quite dead;' and if he is, might not the poor relic of mortality be allowed in mere charity to lie peacefully entombed in his collegiate cloisters? Yet, after all, it is only among the great Anglo-Saxon race that the profession of teaching is without honour; and even among us it may be allowed that it is a mode of earning a pittance as decent and comparatively innocuous as another. We cannot, all of us, taste the fierce joys of writing for the daily or weekly press, and the barrister's 'crowded hours of glorious life' in the law courts would be more overcrowded than ever were not a few *fainéants* suffered to moulder in the retirement of a university. Seriously, it was all very well for the young lions of the Press to denounce the torpor of Dons in the bad old days when colleges were close corporations — when Fellows inherited their bloated revenues without competition, and simply because they happened to be born in a particular corner of some rural district. But now that nearly every First-class man has the chance of election and would be a Fellow if he could, one is tempted to recall the ancient fable of the sour grapes. Or at least the *esprits forts* whom the University has reluctantly driven out into the great world might be grateful to her for saving them in spite of themselves from an existence of futile incapacity.

Probably as long as colleges exist in something like their present form—until the People takes a short way with them, abolishes common rooms and the Long Vacation, and pays college tutors by a system of 'results fees'—these things will continue to be said. Deans and Senior Tutors will never escape the stigma of torpor or incapacity. That quite respectable rhymester, Mr. Robert Montgomery (who, had he not been unlucky enough to cross the path of Lord Macaulay, might have lived and died and been forgotten as the author of metrical works not worse than many that have escaped the lash), has left to the world a long poem—of which the sentiments are always, and the rhymes usually, correct—entitled 'Oxford.' He has taken all Oxford life for his subject, Dons included; and this is how he describes the fate of College Tutors:—

> 'The dunce, the drone, the freshman or the fool,
> 'Tis theirs to counsel, teach, o'erawe, and rule!
> Their only meed—some execrating word
> To blight the hour when first their voice was heard.'

To a certain extent this is true in all ages. But there are worse things than mere sloth: this is not the measure of the crimes charged against college authorities. They —even such contemptible beings as they— are said to have the audacity to neglect untitled merit, and to truckle to the aristocracy. Every one knows Thackeray's terrible indictment of University snobs: Crump, the pompous dignitary (who, to do him justice, seriously thinks himself greater than the Czar of All the Russias), and Hugby, the tutor grovelling before the lordling who has played him a practical joke. Every one remembers how even the late Laureate gibbeted his Dons—how

> 'One
> Discussed his tutor, rough to common men,
> But honeying at the whisper of a lord:
> And one the Master, as a rogue in grain,
> Veneer'd with sanctimonious theory.'

No doubt Universities are not immaculate. There have been Tartuffes and tuft-hunters there, as in the great world. No doubt, too, it was very wrong to allow noblemen to wear badges of their rank, and take their degrees without examination (although the crime was a lesser one in the days before class-lists were, when even the untitled commoner became a Bachelor by dark and disreputable methods); but these things are not done any more. At this day there are probably few places where a title is less regarded than at Oxford or Cambridge. It is true that rumour asserts the existence of certain circles where, *ceteris paribus*, the virtuous proprietor of wealth and a handle to his name is welcomed with more effusion than the equally respectable, but less fortunate, holder of an eleemosynary exhibition. But, after all, even external Society, which regards tuft-hunting with just displeasure, does—it is said — continue to maintain these invidious distinctions when it is sending out invitations to dinner. The fact is that there are a great many peccadilloes in London which become crimes at the University.

Satire, however, does not confine itself to Dons: undergraduates come in for a share of it too, though in a different way. When the novelist condescends to depict the Fellow of a college, it is usually as a person more or less feeble, futile, and generally *manqué*. The Don can never be a hero, but neither is he qualified to play the part of villain; his virtues and his vices are all alike inadequate. If he is bad, his badness is rarely more than contemptible; if he is good, it is in a negative and passionless way, and the great rewards of life are, as a rule, considered as being out of his reach. But with the undergraduate the case is different. He —as we have said—is always in extremes: literature gives him the premier *rôle* either as hero or villain; but it is as the villain that he is the most interesting and picturesque. Satire and fiction generally describe him as an adept in vicious habits. So sings Mr. Robert Montgomery, with admirable propriety:—

'In Oxford see the Reprobate appear!
Big with the promise of a mad career:
With cash and consequence to lead the way,
A fool by night and more than fop by day!'

Over and over again we have the old picture of the Rake's Progress which the world has learnt to know so well: the youth absents himself from his lectures, perhaps even goes to Woodstock (horrid thought!) — 'Woodstock rattles with eternal wheels' is the elegant phrase of Mr. Montgomery—and, in short, plays the fool generally :—

> 'Till night advance, whose reign divine
> Is chastely dedicate to cards and wine.'

The specimen student of the nineteenth century will probably survive in history as represented in these remarkable colours, and the virtuous youth of a hundred years hence will shudder to think of a generation so completely given over to drunkenness, debauchery, and neglect of the Higher Life generally. There is a *naïveté* and directness about undergraduate error which is the easy prey of any satirist ; and curiously enough the public, and even that large class which sends its sons to the Universities, apparently likes to pretend a belief that youth is really brought up in an atmosphere of open and unchecked deviation from the paths of discipline and morality. If Paterfamilias seriously believed that the academic types presented to

PARSON'S PLEASURE. *Drawn by L. Speca.*

him in literature were genuine and frequent phenomena, he would probably send his offspring in for the London Matriculation. But he knows pretty well that the University

is really not rotten to the core, and that colleges are not always ruled by incapables, nor college opinion mainly formed by rakes and spendthrifts; and at the same time it gives the British Public a certain pleasure to imagine that it too has heard the chimes at midnight, although it now goes to bed at half-past ten — that it has been a devil of a fellow in its youth. This fancy is always piquant, and raises a man in his own estimation and that of his friends.

These little inconsistences are of a piece with the whole attitude of the unacademic world towards the Universities. Men come down from London to rest, perhaps, for a day or two from the labours of the Session. They are inspired with a transient enthusiasm for antiquity. They praise academic calm : they affect to wish that they, too, were privileged to live that life of learned leisure which is commonly supposed to be the lot of all Fellows and Tutors. Then they go away, and vote for a new University Commission.

VII

DIARY OF A DON

*'Collegiate life next opens on thy way,
Begins at morn and mingles with the day.'*
R. *Montgomery*.

HALF-PAST SEVEN A.M.: enter my scout, noisily, as one who is accustomed to wake undergraduates. He throws my bath violently on the floor and fills it with ice-cold water. 'What kind of a morning is it?' No better than usual: rain, east wind, occasional snow. *Must* get up nevertheless: haven't superintended a roll-call for three days, and the thing will become a scandal. Never mind: one more snooze.... There are the bells (Oh, those bells!) ringing for a quarter to eight. Ugh!

Dress in the dark, imperfectly: no time to shave. Cap and gown apparently lost. Where the —— Oh, here they are, under the table.

Must try to develop habits of neatness. Somebody else's cap: too big.

Roll-call in full swing in Hall: that is, the college porter is there, ticking off undergraduates' names as they come in. Hall very cold and untidy: college cat scavenging remnants of last night's dinner. Portrait of the Founder looking as if he never expected the college to come to this kind of thing. Men appear in various stages of dishabille. Must make an example of some one: 'Really Mr. Tinkler, I must ask you to put on something besides an ulster.' Tinkler explains that he is fully dressed, opening his ulster and disclosing an elaborate toilet: unfortunate—have to apologise. During the incident several men without caps and gowns succeed in making their escape.

Back in my rooms: finish dressing. Fire out, no hot water. This is what they call the luxurious existence of a College Fellow. Post arrives: chiefly bills and circulars: several notes from undergraduates. 'Dear Sir,—May I go to London for the day in order to keep an important engagement.' Dentist, I suppose. 'Dear Mr. ——,—I am sorry that I was absent from your valuable lecture yesterday, as I was not aware you would do so.' 'Dear Sir,—I shall be much obliged if I may have leave off my lecture this morning, as I wish to go out hunting.' Candid, at any rate. 'Mr. —— presents his compliments to Mr. —— and regrets that he is compelled to be absent from his Latin Prose lecture, because I cannot come.' Simple and convincing. Whip from the Secretary of the Non-Placet Society: urgent request to attend in Convocation and oppose nefarious attempt to insert 'and' in the wording of Stat. Tit. Cap. LXX. 18. Never heard of the statute before. Breakfast.

College cook apparently thinks that a hitherto unimpaired appetite can be satisfied by what seems to be a cold chaffinch on toast. 'Take it away, please, and get me an egg.' Egg arrives: not so old as chaffinch, but nearly: didn't say I wanted a chicken. Scout apologises: must have brought me an undergraduate's egg by mistake. Never mind; plain living and high thinking. Two college servants come to report men absent last night from their rooms. Must have given them leave to go down: can't remember it, though. Matter for investigation. Porter reports gentleman coming into college at 12.10 last night. All right : 'The Dean's compliment's to Mr. ——, and will he please to call upon him at once.' 'Mr. ——'s compliments to the Dean, and he has given orders not to be awakened till ten, but will come when he is dressed.' Obliging.

Lecture to be delivered at ten o'clock to Honours men, on point of ancient custom : very interesting : Time of Roman Dinner, whether at 2.30 or 2.45. Have got copious notes on the subject somewhere : must read them up before lecture, as it never looks well to be in difficulties with your own MS.— looks as if you hadn't the subject at your fingers' ends. Notes can't be found. Know I saw them on my table three weeks ago, and table can't have been dusted since then. Oh, here they are : illegible. Wonder what I meant by all these abbreviations. Never mind : can leave that part out. Five minutes past ten.

Lecture-room pretty full : two or three scholars, with air of superior intelligence : remainder commoners, in attitudes more or less expressive of distracted attention. One man from another college, looking rather *de trop*. Had two out-college men last time : different men, too : disappointing. Begin my dissertation and try to make abstruse subject attractive : 'learning put lightly, like powder in jam.' Wish that scholar No. 1 wouldn't check my remarks by reference to the authority from whom my notes are copied. Why do they teach men German? Second scholar has last number of the 'Classical Review' open before him. Why? Appears afterwards that the 'Review' contains final and satisfying *reductio ad absurdum* of my theory. Man from another college asks if he may go away. Certainly, if he wishes. Explains that he thought this was Mr. ——'s Theology lecture. Seems to have taken twenty minutes to find out his mistake. Wish that two of the commoners could learn to take notes intelligently, and not take down nothing except the unimportant points. Hope they won't reproduce them next week in the schools.

Ten fifty-five : peroration. Interrupted by entrance of lecturer for next hour. Begs pardon : sorry to have interrupted : doesn't go, however. Peroration spoilt. Lecture over: general sense of relief. Go out with the audience, and overhear one of them tell his friend that, after all, it wasn't so bad as last time. Mem., not to go out with audience in future.

Eleven o'clock : lecture for Passmen. Twelve or fifteen young gentlemen all irreproachably dressed in latest style of undergraduate fashion — Norfolk jacket and brown boots indispensable — and all inclined to be cheerfully tolerant of the lecturer's presence *quand même*, regarding him as a necessary nuisance and part of college system. After all there isn't so much to do between eleven and twelve. Some of them can construe, but consider it unbecoming to make any ostentation of knowledge. Conversation at times animated. 'Really, gentlemen, you might keep something to talk about at the next lecture.' Two men appear at 11.25, noisily. Very sorry: have been at another lecture: couldn't get away. General smile of incredulity, joined in by the new arrivals as they find a place in the most crowded part of lecture-room. Every one takes notes diligently, and is careful to burn them at the end of the hour. Translation proceeds rather slowly. Try it myself: difficult to translate Latin comedy with dignity. Give it up and let myself go—play to the gallery. Gallery evidently considers that frivolity on the lecturer's part is inappropriate to the situation. 11.55: 'Won't keep you longer, gentlemen.'

Twelve: time to do a little quiet work before lunch. Gentleman who was out after twelve last night comes to explain. Was detained in a friend's room (reading) and did not know how late it was. In any case is certain he was in before twelve, because he looked at his watch, and is almost sure his watch is fast. Fined and warned not to do it again: exit grumbling. No more interruptions, I hope. . . . . Boy from the Clarendon Press: editor wants something for the 'Oxford Magazine,' at once: not less than a column: messenger will wait while I write it. Very considerate. Try to write something: presence of boy embarrassing. Ask him to go outside and wait on the staircase. Does so, and continues to whistle 'Daisy Bell,' with accompaniment on the banisters *obbligato*. Composition difficult and result not satisfactory: hope no one will read it. Column nearly finished: man comes to explain why he wants to be absent during three weeks of next term. *Would* he mind going away and calling some other time? Very well: when? Oh, any time, only not now. This is what they call the leisure and philosophic calm of collegiate life.

Lunch in Common Room: cold, clammy, and generally unappetising. Guest who is apparently an old member of the college greets me and says he supposes I've forgotten him. 'Not at all: remember you quite well: glad to meet you again.' Haven't the faintest idea what his name is: awkward. Appears in course of conversation to be ex-undergraduate whom I knew very well and did not like. Evidently regards me as a venerable fossil: he himself has grown bald and fat and looks fifty, more or less: suppose I must be about seventy or eighty. Vice-Principal wants to know if I will play fives at two: yes, if he likes. No, by the way, can't; have got to go and vote in Convocation. Don't know what it is about, but promised to go: can't think why. Time to go.

In the Convocation House. Very few people there, nobody at all interested. Borrow Gazette and study list of agenda. Question on which I promised to vote comes on late, all sorts of uninteresting matters to be settled first: mostly small money grants for scientific purposes: pleasant way of wasting three-quarters of an hour. My question here at last: prepare to die in last ditch in defence of original form of statute. Member of Hebdomadal Council makes inaudible speech, apparently on the subject. No one else has anything to say:

Council's proposal, whatever it is, carried *nem. con.* No voting : might as well have played fives after all : next time shall.

Time for walk round the Parks : rain and mud. Worst of the Parks is, you always meet people of houses where you ought to have called and haven't. Free fight under Rugby rules going on between University and somewhere else. Watch it : don't understand game : try to feel patriotic : can't. . . . . . Meeting at four to oppose introduction of Hawaiian as an optional language in Responsions. Not select : imprudent for a caucus to transact business by inviting its opponents : people of all sorts of opinions present. Head of House makes highly respectable speech, explaining that while qualified support of reform is conceivable and even under possible circumstances advisable, premature action is rarely consistent with mature deliberation. Nobody seems to have anything definite to suggest : most people move amendments. Safe to vote against all of them : difficult to know how you are voting, however : wording of amendments so confusing. All of them

LAWN TENNIS AT OXFORD. *Drawn by Lancelot Speed.*

negatived : substantive motion proposed : lost as well. Question referred to a Committee : ought to have been done at first. Hour and a half wasted. Remember that I have cut my five-o'clock pupil for second time running. Am offered afternoon tea : thirsty, but must be off : man at half-past five. On the way back meet resident sportsman in the High. Has been out with hounds and had best twenty-five minutes of the season, in the afternoon, three miles off. Might have been there myself if it hadn't been for Convocation : hang Convocation ! Never mind ; satisfaction of a good conscience : shall always be able to say that I lost best run of season through devotion to duty.

Six forty-five : pupils gone ; dress for seven-o'clock dinner with friend at St. Anselm's. Man comes to ask why he has been gated : explain : man not satisfied. Gone, at any rate. Another man, asking leave to be out after twelve. Five minutes to dress and walk a quarter of a mile. Wish men wouldn't choose this time for coming to see one. Very late : dinner already begun : no soup, thanks. Meaty atmosphere : noisy atmosphere at lower end of Hall: undergraduates throw bread about. No one in evening dress but myself. Distinguished guest in shape of eminent German Professor: have got next him somehow: wish I hadn't: wears flannel shirt and evidently regards me as a mere butterfly of fashion. Speaks hardly any English: try him in German: replies after an unusual effort on my part, 'Ich spreche nur Deutsch.' My command of the language evidently less complete than I thought: or perhaps he only speaks his own patois. Man opposite me Demonstrator at the Museum, who considers that the University and the world in general was made for physiologists.

Small party in Common Room, most of diners having to see pupils or attend meetings. Will I have any wine? No one else drinks any and my host is a teetotaller: 'No, thanks— never drink wine after dinner.' Truth only a conventional virtue after all. Eminent Teuton would like more beer, but has been long enough in England to know better than to ask for it. Am put next to Demonstrator, who endeavours to give general ideas of digestive organs of a frog, interpreting occasionally in German for Professor's benefit: illustrates with fragments of dessert: most interesting, I am sure. Nothing like the really good talk of an Oxford Common Room, after all. Senior Fellow drinks whisky and water and goes to sleep. Coffee and cigarettes: or will I have a weed? 'Thanks, but must be off: man at nine. . .' Back in college: rooms dark: can't find my matches and fall over furniture.

Man comes to read me an essay. Know nothing about the subject: thought he was going to write on something else. Essay finished: must say something: try to find fault with his facts. Man confronts me with array of statistics, apparently genuine: if so nothing more to say. Criticise his grammar: man offended. Interview rather painful, till concluded by entrance of nine-thirty man with Latin prose. Rather superior young man, who considers himself a scholar. Suggest that part of his vocabulary is not according to classical usage: proves me wrong by reference to dictionary.

Is not surprised to find me mistaken. Wish that Higher Education had stopped in Board Schools and not got down to undergraduates.

Man at ten, with a desire to learn. Stays till near eleven discussing his chances in the schools at great length. Presently comes to his prospects in life. Would send me to sleep if he wouldn't ask me questions.

Eleven: no more men, thank goodness. Tobacco and my lecture for to-morrow. . . . Never could understand why a gentleman being neither intoxicated nor in the society of his friends, cannot cross the quadrangle without a view-halloo. . . There he is again: must go out and see what is going on. Quadrangle very cold, raining. Group of men playing football in the corner: friends look on and encourage them from windows above. As I come on the scene all disappear, with shouts: none identified: saves future trouble, at all events. More tobacco and period of comparative peace. Bedtime.

Wish my scout wouldn't hide hard things under the mattress.

Noise in quadrangle renewed : 'Daddy wouldn't buy me a Bow-wow,' with variations. . . . Some one's oak apparently battered with a poker. *Ought* to get up and go out to stop it. . . .

VIII

THE UNIVERSITY AS A PLACE OF LEARNED LEISURE.

'I had been used for thirty years to no interruption save the tinkling of the dinner-bell and the chapel-bell.'

Essays of Vicesimus Knox.

STANDING with one foot in the Middle Ages and the other in a luxuriously furnished Common Room'—such is Oxford life as summarised by a German visitor, who appears to have been a good deal perplexed, like the outer world in general, by the academic mixture of things ancient and modern, and a host who wore a cap and gown over his evening dress. Certainly the University is a strange medley of contraries. It never seems to be quite clear whether we are going too fast or too slow. We are always reforming something, yet are continually reproached with irrational conservatism. Change and permanence are side by side — permanence that looks as if it could defy time :

'The form remains, the function never dies,'

and yet all the while the change is rapid and complete. Men go down, and are as if they had never been : as is the race of leaves so is that of undergraduates ; and so transiently are they linked with the enduring existence of their University, that, except in the case of the minority who have done great deeds on the river or the cricket-field, they either pass immediately out of recollection or else remain only as a dim and distant tradition of bygone ages. An undergraduate's memory is very short. For him the history of the University is comprised in the three or four years of his own residence. Those who came before him and those who come after are alike separated from him by a great gulf; his predecessors are infinitely older, and his successors immeasurably younger. It makes no difference what his relations to them may be in after-life. Jones, who went down in '74, may be an undistinguished country parson or a struggling junior at the Bar; and Brown, who came up in '75, may be a bishop or a Q.C. with his fortune made; but all the same Brown will always regard Jones as belonging to the almost forgotten heroic period before he came up, and Jones, whatever may be his respect for Brown's undoubted talents, must always to a certain extent feel the paternal interest of a veteran watching the development of youthful promise. So complete is the severance of successive generations, that it is hard to see how undergraduate custom and tradition and College characteristics should have a chance of surviving; yet somehow they do manage to preserve an unbroken continuity. Once give a College a good or a bad name, and that name will stick to it. Plant a custom and it will flourish, defying statutes and Royal Commissions. Conservatism is in the air; even convinced Radicals (in politics) cannot escape from it, and are sometimes Tories in matters relating to their University. They will change the constitution of the realm, but will not stand any tampering with the Hebdomadal Council. Whatever be the reason —whether it be Environment or Heredity— Universities go on doing the same things, only in different ways; they retain that indefinable habit of thought which seems to cling to old grey walls and the shade of ancient elms, which the public calls 'academic' when it is only contemptuous, explaining the word as meaning 'provincial with a difference' when it is angry.

There is the same kind of unalterableness about the few favoured individuals to whom the spirit of the age has allowed a secure and permanent residence in Oxford; a happy class which is now almost limited to Heads of Houses and College servants. You scarcely ever see a scout bearing the outward and visible signs of advancing years; age cannot wither them, nor (it should be added) can custom stale their infinite variety of mis-serving their masters. Perhaps it is they who are the repositories of tradition.

And even Fellows contrive to retain some of the characteristics of their more permanent predecessors, whom we have now learnt to regard as abuses. Hard-worked though they are, and precarious of tenure, they are, nevertheless, in some sort imbued with that flavour of humanity and *dolce far niente* which continues to haunt even a Common Room where Fellows drink nothing but water, and only dine together once a fortnight.

For times are sadly changed now, and a fellowship is far from being the haven of rest which it once was, and still is to a few. Look at that old Fellow pacing with slow and leisurely steps beneath Magdalen or Christchurch elms: regard him well, for he is an interesting survival, and presently he and his kind will be nothing but a memory, and probably the progressive spirit of democracy will hold him up as an awful example. He is a link with a practically extinct period. When he was first elected *verus et perpetuus socius* of his college — without examination — the University of Oxford was in a parlous state.

Reform was as yet unheard of, or only loomed dimly in the distance. Noblemen still wore tufts—think how that would scandalise us now!—and 'gentlemen commoners' came up with the declared and recognised intention of living as gentlemen commoners should. Except for the invention of the examination system —and the demon of the schools was satisfied with only a mouthful of victims then—Oxford of the forties had not substantially changed since the last century—since the days when Mr. Gibbon was a gentleman commoner at Magdalen College, where his excuses for cutting his lectures in the morning were 'received with a smile,' and where he found himself horribly bored by the 'private scandal' and 'dull and deep potations' of the seniors with whom he was invited to associate in the evening. Not much had changed since those days: lectures were still disciplinary exercises rather than vehicles of instruction, and the vespertinal port was rarely if ever interrupted in its circulation by 'the man who comes at nine.' Many holders of fellowships scarcely came near the University; those who did reside were often not much concerned about the instruction of undergraduates, and still less with 'intercollegiate competition.' Perhaps it was not their life's work: a fellowship might be only a stepping-stone to a college living, when a sufficiently fat benefice should fall vacant and allow the dean or subwarden to marry and retire into the country; and even the don who meant to be a don all his days put study or learned leisure first and instruction second, the world not yet believing in the 'spoon-feeding' of youth. Very often, of course, they did nothing. After all, when you pay a man for exercising no particular functions, you can scarcely blame him for strictly fulfilling the conditions under which he was elected. 'But what do they do?' inquired—quite recently—a tourist, pointing to the fellows' buildings of a certain college. 'Do?!!' replied the Oxford cicerone—'do? . . . why them's fellows!' But if there was inactivity, it is only the more credit to the minority who really did interest themselves in the work of their pupils. Not that the relation of authorities to undergraduates was ever then what it has since become—whether the change be for the better or the worse. Few attempts were made to bridge the chasm which must always yawn between the life of teacher and taught. Perhaps now the attempt is a little over-emphasised; certainly things are done which would have made each particular hair to stand on end on the head of a Fellow of the old school. In his solemn and formal way he winked at rowing, considering it rather fast and on the whole an inevitable sign of declining morals. He wore his cap and gown with the anachronistic persistency of Mr. Toole in 'The Don,' and sighed over the levity of a colleague who occasionally sported a blue coat with brass buttons. Had you told him that within the present century College Tutors would be seen in flannels, and that a Head of a House could actually row on the river in an eight — albeit the ship in question be manned by comparatively grave and reverend seniors, yclept the Ancient Mariners

—he would probably have replied in the formula ascribed to Dr. Johnson : 'Let me tell you, sir, that in order to be what you consider humorous it is not necessary that you should be also indecent!' But there is a lower depth still ; and grave dignitaries of the University have been seen riding bicycles.

All this would have been quite unintelligible to the youthful days of our friend, whom we see leisurely approaching the evening of his days in the midst of a generation that does not know him indeed, but which is certainly benefited by his presence and the picture of academic repose which he displays to his much-troubled and harassed successors : a peaceful, cloistered life ; soon to leave nothing behind it but a brass in the College chapel, a few Common Room anecdotes, and a vague tradition, perhaps, of a ghost on the old familiar staircase. Far different is the lot of the Fellow *fin de siècle*; 'by many names men know him,' whether he be the holder of an 'official' Fellowship, or a 'Prize Fellow' who is entitled to his emoluments only for the paltry period of seven years. And what emoluments! Verily the mouth of Democracy must water at the thought of the annual 'division of the spoils' which used to take place under the old *régime:* spoils which were worth dividing, too, in the days when rents were paid without a murmur, and colleges had not as yet to allow tenants to hold at half-a-crown an acre, lest the farm should be unlet altogether. But now if a Prize Fellow receives his 200*l.* a year he may consider himself lucky ; and remember that if he is not blessed with this world's goods, the grim humours of the last Commission at least allowed him the inestimable privilege of marrying—on 200*l.* a year. After all, it is not every one who receives even that salary for doing nothing.

The 'official' variety of Fellow, or the Prize Fellow who chooses to be a College Tutor, is a schoolmaster, with a difference. He has rather longer holidays—if he can afford to enjoy them—and a considerably shorter purse than the instructors of youth at some great schools. He is so far unfortunate in his predecessors, that he has inherited the reputation of the Fellows of old time. Everybody else is working: the Fellow is still a useless drone. As a matter of fact, the unfortunate man is always doing something — working vehemently with a laudable desire to get that into eight weeks which should properly take twelve; or taking his recreation violently, riding forty miles on a bicycle, with a spurt at the finish so as not to miss his five-o'clock pupil ; sitting on interminable committees—everything in Oxford is managed by a committee, partly, perhaps, because 'Boards are very often screens ;' or sitting upon a disorderly undergraduate. On the whole, the kicks are many, and the halfpence comparatively few. He has the Long Vacation, of course, but then he is always employed in writing his lectures for next term, or compiling a school edition, or a handbook, or an abridgment of somebody else's school edition or handbook, in order to keep the pot boiling—more especially if he has fallen a victim to matrimony, and established himself in the red-brick part of Oxford. It is true that there is the prospect—on paper—of a pension when he is past his work, but in the present state of College finances that is not exactly a vista of leisured opulence. Altogether there is not very much repose about *him*. College Tutors in these days are expected to work. It is on record that a tourist from a manufacturing district on seeing four tutors snatching a brief hour at lawn-tennis, remarked, 'I suppose there's *another shift* working inside?' Such are the requirements of the age and the manufacturing districts.

Nor are beer and skittles unadulterated the lot of the undergraduate either—whatever the impression that his sisters and cousins may derive from the gaieties of the Eights and 'Commem.' For the spirit of the century and the 'Sturm und Drang' of a restless world has got hold of the 'Man,' too, and will not suffer him to live quite so peacefully as the Verdant Greens and Bouncers of old. Everybody must do something; they must be 'up and doing,' or else they have a good chance of finding themselves 'sent down.' I do not speak of the reading man, who naturally finds his vocation in a period of activity—but rather of the man who is by nature non-reading, and has to sacrifice his natural desires to the pressure of public opinion acting through his tutor. Perhaps he is made to go in for honours; but even if he reads only for a pass, the schools are always with him—he is always being pulled up to see how he is growing; or at least he must be serving his College in one way or another — if not by winning distinction in the schools, by toiling on the river or the cricket-field. Then he is expected to interest himself in all the movements of the last quarter of the nineteenth century; he must belong to several societies; he cannot even be properly idle without forming himself into an association for the purpose. If he wants to make a practice of picnicing on the Cherwell he founds a 'Cherwell Lunch Club,' with meetings, no doubt, and possibly an 'organ' to advocate his highly meritorious views. An excellent and a healthy life, no doubt! but yet one is tempted sometimes to fear that the loafer may become extinct; and then where are our poets to come from? For it is a great thing to be able to loaf well: it softens the manners and does not allow them to be fierce; and there is no place for it like the streams and gardens of an ancient University. If a man does not learn the great art of doing nothing there, he will never acquire it anywhere else; and it is there, and in the summer term, that this laudable practice will probably survive when it is unknown even in Government Offices.

For there is a season of the year when even the sternest scholar or athlete and the most earnest promoter of Movements yields to the *genius loci;* when the summer term is drawing to a close, and the May east winds have yielded to the warmth of June, and the lilacs and laburnums are blossoming in College gardens; when the shouting and the glory and the bonfires of the Eights are over, and the invasion of Commemoration has not yet begun. Then, if ever, is the time for doing nothing. Then the unwilling victim of lectures shakes off his chains and revels in a temporary freedom, not unconnected with the fact that his tutor has gone for a picnic to Nuneham. Perhaps he has been rowing in his College Eight, and is entitled to repose on the laurels of 'six bumps;' perhaps he is not in the schools himself, and can afford to pity the unfortunates who are. And how many are the delightful ways of loafing! You may propel the object of your affections — if she is up, as she very often is at this time — in a punt on that most academic stream, the Cherwell, while Charles (your friend) escorts the chaperon in a dingey some little distance in front; you may lie lazily in the sun in Worcester or St. John's gardens, with a novel, or a friend, or both; you may search Bagley and Powderhill for late bluebells, and fancy that you have found 'high on its heathy ridge' the tree known to Arnold and Clough.

Or if you are more enterprising you may travel further afield and explore the high beech woods of the Chiltern slopes and the bare, breezy uplands of the Berkshire downs; but this, perhaps, demands more energy than belongs to the truly conscientious loafer.

Well, let the idle undergraduate make the most of his time now; it is not likely that he will be able to loaf in after-life. Nor (for the matter of that) will his successors be allowed to take their ease here in Oxford even in the summer, in those happy days when the University is to be turned into an industrial school, and a place for the education no longer of the English gentleman but the British citizen. Will that day ever come? The spirit of the age is determined that it shall. But perhaps the spirit of the place may be too much for it yet.

London: Strangeways, Printers.

www.ingramcontent.com/pod-product-compliance
Lightning Source LLC
Chambersburg PA
CBHW032150160426
43197CB00008B/852